"This series is a tremendous resource for those wanting to study and teach the Bible with an understanding of how the gospel is woven throughout Scripture. Here are gospel-minded pastors and scholars doing gospel business from all the Scriptures. This is a biblical and theological feast preparing God's people to apply the entire Bible to all of life with heart and mind wholly committed to Christ's priorities."

BRYAN CHAPELL, President Emeritus, Covenant Theological Seminary; Senior Pastor, Grace Presbyterian Church, Peoria, Illinois

"Mark Twain may have smiled when he wrote to a friend, 'I didn't have time to write you a short letter, so I wrote you a long letter.' But the truth of Twain's remark remains serious and universal, because well-reasoned, compact writing requires extra time and extra hard work. And this is what we have in the Crossway Bible study series *Knowing the Bible*. The skilled authors and notable editors provide the contours of each book of the Bible as well as the grand theological themes that bind them together as one Book. Here, in a 12-week format, are carefully wrought studies that will ignite the mind and the heart."

R. KENT HUGHES, Visiting Professor of Practical Theology, Westminster Theological Seminary

"*Knowing the Bible* brings together a gifted team of Bible teachers to produce a high-quality series of study guides. The coordinated focus of these materials is unique: biblical content, provocative questions, systematic theology, practical application, and the gospel story of God's grace presented all the way through Scripture."

PHILIP G. RYKEN, President, Wheaton College

"These *Knowing the Bible* volumes provide a significant and very welcome variation on the general run of inductive Bible studies. This series provides substantial instruction, as well as teaching through the very questions that are asked. *Knowing the Bible* then goes even further by showing how any given text links with the gospel, the whole Bible, and the formation of theology. I heartily endorse this orientation of individual books to the whole Bible and the gospel, and I applaud the demonstration that sound theology was not something invented later by Christians, but is right there in the pages of Scripture."

GRAEME L. GOLDSWORTHY, former lecturer, Moore Theological College; author, *According to Plan, Gospel and Kingdom, The Gospel in Revelation,* and *Gospel and Wisdom*

"What a gift to earnest, Bible-loving, Bible-searching believers! The organization and structure of the Bible study format presented through the *Knowing the Bible* series is so well conceived. Students of the Word are led to understand the content of passages through perceptive, guided questions, and they are given rich insights and application all along the way in the brief but illuminating sections that conclude each study. What potential growth in depth and breadth of understanding these studies offer! One can only pray that vast numbers of believers will discover more of God and the beauty of his Word through these rich studies."

BRUCE A. WARE, Professor of Christian Theology, The Southern Baptist Theological Seminary

T0326658

KNOWING THE BIBLE

J. I. Packer, Theological Editor
Dane C. Ortlund, Series Editor
Lane T. Dennis, Executive Editor

•   •   •   •   •   •

Genesis	Psalms	Jonah, Micah, and Nahum	Ephesians
Exodus	Proverbs		Philippians
Leviticus	Ecclesiastes	Haggai, Zechariah, and Malachi	Colossians and Philemon
Numbers	Song of Solomon		
Deuteronomy	Isaiah	Matthew	1–2 Thessalonians
Joshua	Jeremiah	Mark	1–2 Timothy and Titus
Judges	Lamentations, Habakkuk, and Zephaniah	Luke	
Ruth and Esther		John	Hebrews
1–2 Samuel	Ezekiel	Acts	James
1–2 Kings	Daniel	Romans	1–2 Peter and Jude
1–2 Chronicles	Hosea	1 Corinthians	1–3 John
Ezra and Nehemiah	Joel, Amos, and Obadiah	2 Corinthians	Revelation
Job		Galatians	

•   •   •   •   •   •

J. I. PACKER was the former Board of Governors' Professor of Theology at Regent College (Vancouver, BC). Dr. Packer earned his DPhil at the University of Oxford. He is known and loved worldwide as the author of the best-selling book *Knowing God*, as well as many other titles on theology and the Christian life. He served as the General Editor of the ESV Bible and as the Theological Editor for the *ESV Study Bible*.

LANE T. DENNIS is CEO of Crossway, a not-for-profit publishing ministry. Dr. Dennis earned his PhD from Northwestern University. He is Chair of the ESV Bible Translation Oversight Committee and Executive Editor of the *ESV Study Bible*.

DANE C. ORTLUND (PhD, Wheaton College) serves as senior pastor of Naperville Presbyterian Church in Naperville, Illinois. He is an editor for the Knowing the Bible series and the Short Studies in Biblical Theology series, and is the author of several books, including *Gentle and Lowly: The Heart of Christ for Sinners and Sufferers*.

PROVERBS

A 12-WEEK STUDY

Lydia Brownback

:: CROSSWAY®

WHEATON, ILLINOIS

Trade paperback ISBN: 978-1-4335-4022-6
ePub ISBN: 978-1-4335-4025-7
PDF ISBN: 978-1-4335-4023-3
Mobipocket ISBN: 978-1-4335-4024-0

Crossway is a publishing ministry of Good News Publishers.

VP		31	30	29	28	27	26	25	24
20	19	18	17	16	15	14	13	12	11

TABLE OF CONTENTS

SERIES PREFACE

KNOWING THE BIBLE, as the series title indicates, was created to help readers know and understand the meaning, the message, and the God of the Bible. Each volume in the series consists of 12 units that progressively take the reader through a clear, concise study of that book of the Bible. In this way, any given volume can fruitfully be used in a 12-week format either in group study, such as in a church-based context, or in individual study. Of course, these 12 studies could be completed in fewer or more than 12 weeks, as convenient, depending on the context in which they are used.

Each study unit gives an overview of the text at hand before digging into it with a series of questions for reflection or discussion. The unit then concludes by highlighting the gospel of grace in each passage ("Gospel Glimpses"), identifying whole-Bible themes that occur in the passage ("Whole-Bible Connections"), and pinpointing Christian doctrines that are affirmed in the passage ("Theological Soundings").

The final component to each unit is a section for reflecting on personal and practical implications from the passage at hand. The layout provides space for recording responses to the questions proposed, and we think readers need to do this to get the full benefit of the exercise. The series also includes definitions of key words. These definitions are indicated by a note number in the text and are found at the end of each chapter.

Lastly, to help understand the Bible in this deeper way, we urge readers to use the ESV Bible and the *ESV Study Bible*, which are available in various print and digital formats, including online editions at esv.org. The Knowing the Bible series is also available online.

May the Lord greatly bless your study as you seek to know him through knowing his Word.

J. I. Packer
Lane T. Dennis

WEEK 1: OVERVIEW

▲

Proverbs is a collection or anthology of individual proverbs that offers skill in the art of godly living. The book provides wisdom for reflecting God's glory in the details of daily life and in one's relationships. It demonstrates clearly that God's ways are intensely practical and apply to every aspect of his people's lives. The main emphasis of the book is to show that relating rightly to God involves, first, seeking to understand his truth, and second, embracing and obeying that truth. Clear throughout is that following God's paths leads to blessing, whereas forsaking them leads to ruin.

Proverbs, along with Job, Ecclesiastes, and Song of Solomon, is part of the Old Testament "Wisdom Literature." The first nine chapters of Proverbs are wisdom poems urging readers to pursue wisdom, and this sets the stage for how to read and apply the remainder of the book, chapters 10–31, which contain mostly concise statements that contrast wise and foolish choices. These contrasts are observations of how God has designed the world to work; they should not be taken as promises.

There are four primary characters in Proverbs: the wise, the fool, the simple, and the scoffer. The wise embrace God's covenant. Fools, on the other hand, are opposed to God, yet they are not beyond hope. The simple are those who remain uncommitted to either wisdom or folly, and because of that they are easily misled. Scoffers are proud and arrogant and scorn God's ways. Other voices in the book include Lady Wisdom and Lady Folly, each of whom personifies[1] the characteristics of her name, and the Woman of Excellence, with whom the book concludes.

Placing It in the Larger Story

Proverbs advances the overarching theme of the Bible, which is God's calling, preserving, and shaping a people for himself. Proverbs advances this theme uniquely through the offer of God-centered wisdom. In the four poems of chapters 1–9, wisdom is personified as a noble lady whom one should pursue. The personification anticipates the words of the apostle Paul: "Jews demand signs and Greeks seek wisdom, but we preach Christ crucified, a stumbling block to Jews and folly to Gentiles, but to those who are called, both Jews and Greeks, Christ the power of God and the wisdom of God" (1 Cor. 1:22–24).

Key Verse

"The fear of the LORD is the beginning of knowledge; fools despise wisdom and instruction." (Prov. 1:7)

Date and Historical Background

King Solomon (c. 971–931 BC) is the author of many of the proverbs, and he gave oversight to the rest of the collection. His pursuit of wisdom and his interest in proverbs is verified in the Historical Books of Scripture (e.g., 1 Kings 4:29–34). Compiling proverbs and discourses on wisdom was a common practice in the ancient world, but only this collection bases its wisdom on the fear of the Lord, Yahweh (God's covenant[2] name). The present form of the book dates to a later time than the reign of Solomon, but the collection as a whole bears his stamp.

Outline

   I. Goal and Motto (1:1–7)

  II. A Father's Invitation to Wisdom (1:8–9:18)

     A. First paternal appeal: do not join those greedy for unjust gain (1:8–19)

     B. First wisdom appeal (1:20–33)

C. Second paternal appeal: get wisdom (2:1–22)

D. Third paternal appeal: fear the Lord (3:1–12)

E. A hymn to wisdom (3:13–20)

F. Fourth paternal appeal: walk securely in wisdom (3:21–35)

G. Fifth paternal appeal: wisdom is a tradition worth maintaining (4:1–9)

H. Sixth paternal appeal: the two ways (4:10–19)

I. Seventh paternal appeal: maintain a heart of wisdom (4:20–27)

J. Eighth paternal appeal: good and bad sexuality (5:1–23)

K. Warnings relating to securing debt, sloth, and sowing discord (6:1–19)

L. Ninth paternal appeal: adultery leads to ruin (6:20–35)

M. Tenth paternal appeal: keep away from temptations to adultery (7:1–27)

N. Second wisdom appeal (8:1–36)

O. Lady Wisdom and Lady Folly (9:1–18)

III. Proverbs of Solomon (10:1–22:16)

IV. The Thirty Sayings of "the Wise" (22:17–24:22)

V. Further Sayings of "the Wise" (24:23–34)

VI. Hezekiah's Collection of Solomonic Proverbs (25:1–29:27)

VII. The Sayings of Agur (30:1–33)

VIII. The Sayings of King Lemuel (31:1–9)

IX. An Alphabet of Womanly Excellence (31:10–31)

▶ As You Get Started . . .

What is your understanding of how the book of Proverbs advances the story-line of the Bible?

How does the historical context in which Proverbs was originally compiled shape our understanding of the book?

How should we understand the personification of wisdom in Proverbs 8–9?

As You Finish This Unit . . .

Take a few minutes to ask God to humble your heart—to deepen your "fear of the Lord"—so that you will embrace the wisdom he offers in Proverbs.

Definitions

[1] **Personification** – Rhetorical device attributing human characteristics to nonhuman things, such as animals, plants, or objects. An example is found in Isaiah 55:12: "The mountains and the hills before you shall break forth into singing, and all the trees of the field shall clap their hands."

[2] **Covenant** – A binding agreement between two parties, typically involving a formal statement of their relationship, a list of stipulations and obligations for both parties, a list of witnesses to the agreement, and a list of curses for unfaithfulness and blessings for faithfulness to the agreement. The Old Testament is more properly understood as the old covenant, meaning the agreement established between God and his people prior to the coming of Jesus Christ and the establishment of the new covenant (New Testament).

WEEK 2: THE BEGINNING OF KNOWLEDGE

Proverbs 1:1–7

▲

The Place of the Passage

This brief passage sets the stage for the whole book of Proverbs. Verse 1 shows that the instruction contained in the collection is authoritative for God's people because it comes from God's appointed king, Solomon, son of David. Verses 2–6 describe the goal of the book, which is the acquisition of wisdom and knowledge, and verse 7 reveals what makes this acquisition possible: "The fear of the LORD is the beginning of knowledge" (v. 7).

The Big Picture

Proverbs 1:1–7 shows us that humble, reverent submission to the covenant Lord is the path to covenant life.

Reflection and Discussion

Read through the complete passage for this study, Proverbs 1:1–7. Then review the questions below concerning this introductory section to Proverbs and write your notes on them. (For further background, see the *ESV Study Bible*, page 1135, or visit esv.org.)

When Solomon succeeded his father, David, as king of Israel, he prayed for wisdom to govern God's people, and God granted his request (1 Kings 3:5–12). As a result, Israel flourished under Solomon's leadership for many years. The practice of writing and compiling proverbs crossed cultural lines in the ancient world, but Solomon's collection is distinctive in that it identifies submission to the Lord as the source of true wisdom. In light of these historical facts, how is God's covenant with his people reflected in the introductory verse, "The proverbs of Solomon, son of David" (Prov. 1:1)?

"To know . . . to understand . . . to receive . . . to give." Proverbs 1:2–5 provides the purpose and benefits of the book. Those who take its instruction to heart will develop an increasing sensitivity to that which is practically, intellectually, and morally wise. What heart posture is indicated in these verses as necessary to know, receive, and understand?

"To give prudence to the simple" (Prov. 1:4a). The benefits of wisdom are held out to the simple. The *simple* in Proverbs are those not firmly committed either to wisdom or to folly, and because of that, they do not apply themselves to the discipline needed to gain and grow in wisdom. Why do you think such a person is vulnerable to danger?

"To give prudence to the simple, knowledge and discretion to the youth" (Prov. 1:4). Much of the instruction in Proverbs is issued to young men in Israel, the next generation of leaders of covenant life. Several sections in the first nine chapters begin with a similar refrain: "Hear, O sons, a father's instruction" (4:1; compare 1:8; 2:1; 3:1; 5:1; 6:1, 20; 7:1, 24; 8:32). Read Deuteronomy 4:9–10, a portion of Moses' instruction to the Israelites as they prepared to enter the Promised Land. How do the father-to-son admonitions in Proverbs take their place within Moses' instruction?

"Let the wise hear and increase in learning, and the one who understands obtain guidance" (Prov. 1:5). What can we infer from the fact that wisdom is offered to those who are already wise?

We're told in Proverbs 1:6 that the wise are able to understand riddles. We find riddles elsewhere in Scripture. Ezekiel, for example, issues an oracle using a riddle in chapter 17 of his prophecy, and a riddle is put forth in Psalm 49:4–6. Why do you think Scripture uses riddles as a teaching device?

"The fear of the LORD" (Prov. 1:7a). This phrase occurs frequently in Proverbs and is sprinkled throughout the Old Testament and found twice in the New Testament. Read Job 28:28; Psalm 19:9; Isaiah 11:2–3; Acts 9:31; and 2 Corinthians 5:11, as well as the surrounding context of these verses, and then describe what it means to "fear the Lord."

"The fear of the LORD is the beginning of knowledge" (Prov. 1:7a). This verse summarizes the message of the entire book. The quest for wisdom begins with the fear of the Lord (see 9:10 and Ps. 111:10). Knowledge and wisdom are closely tied together in Proverbs. Knowledge has to do with developing a correct understanding of the world, while wisdom is the acquired skill of applying that knowledge rightly. Why do you think the fear of the Lord is a prerequisite for obtaining knowledge and wisdom?

"Fools despise wisdom and instruction" (Prov. 1:7b). The contrast is between the way of wisdom and the way of folly. This contrast dominates the entire book. The way of wisdom, the fear of the Lord, is set against the way of folly, which in Proverbs is equated with evil. What heart attitude revealed here classifies someone as a fool?

Read through the following three sections on *Gospel Glimpses, Whole-Bible Connections*, and *Theological Soundings*. Then take time to consider the *Personal Implications* these sections may have for you.

▶ Gospel Glimpses

WISDOM REVEALED. The covenant Lord condescends to reveal his wisdom, not only to the wise but also to the simple and the fool, so that each might live in joyful fellowship with him and with one another. Each is unworthy of this gift—even the wise—yet wisdom and its benefits are offered for the taking.

TRANSFORMING GRACE. This opening passage of Proverbs, which outlines the transformative nature of wisdom, points forward to the believer's sanctification[1] in Christ. The apostle Paul wrote that believers are progressively transformed by the Holy Spirit into Christ's likeness as they behold the glory of Jesus Christ (2 Cor. 3:18).

EARS TO HEAR. "Let the wise hear and increase in learning, and the one who understands obtain guidance" (Prov. 1:5). Both the call to hear and the ability to do so are gracious gifts from God. Many times in the Gospels Jesus issues a call to hear, saying, "He who has ears to hear, let him hear," and we find a gracious call to hear in Revelation: "He who has an ear, let him hear what the Spirit says to the churches" (2:7, 11, 17, 29; 3:6, 13, 22).

Whole-Bible Connections

DAVIDIC KING. The Lord made a promise to King David: "I will raise up your offspring after you, who shall come from your body, and I will establish his kingdom. He shall build a house for my name, and I will establish the throne of his kingdom forever. I will be to him a father, and he shall be to me a son" (2 Sam. 7:12–14). The offspring spoken of in this promise is Solomon, the author-compiler of Proverbs. Later, Hebrews 1:5 applies the words "I will be to him a father, and he shall be to me a son" to Christ.

FEAR OF THE LORD. Throughout Scripture the fear of the Lord is prescribed for God's people. It involves both reverent awe and a healthy fear of God's displeasure and discipline. In Acts it refers either to godly awe, reverence, and devotion (see Acts 2:43; 10:2; 13:26) or to fear of God's displeasure and fatherly discipline. In Romans 3:18 Paul identifies the root cause of sin as a failure to fear and honor God, and he makes his case from Psalm 36:1: "There is no fear of God before their eyes." Any society that commonly assumes that God will not discipline sin in this life or judge it in the next has no fear of God and will therefore give itself increasingly to evil. Such people are labeled as "fools" and "scoffers" in Proverbs.

Theological Soundings

SANCTIFICATION. Proverbs' introductory passage makes clear that growth in godly character is not an automatic process. The way of wisdom is held out to us, but we must expose ourselves to its instruction in order to manifest it: "Let the wise hear and increase in learning" (Prov. 1:5). Here we get a glimpse of sanctification, the process of being made holy, which is revealed more fully in the New Testament. The Word, the Spirit, and the believer all participate in this transformation process. We see this joint action in Romans 12:2: "Do not be conformed to this world, but be transformed by the renewal of your mind"; and again in Philippians 2:12–13: "Work out your own salvation with fear and trembling, for it is God who works in you, both to will and to work for his good pleasure."

SCRIPTURE. The fear of the Lord, what generates knowledge and wisdom, comes by studying and obeying the Word of God.[2] All God's people are to be open and submissive to its instruction. The transformative power of God's Word has been emphasized ever since the law was given by God to Moses: "Now this is the commandment—the statutes and the rules—that the LORD your God commanded me to teach you . . . that you may fear the LORD your God, you and your son and your son's son, by keeping all his statutes and his commandments . . . that your days may be long" (Deut. 6:1–2); and it continues into the new covenant era: "All Scripture is breathed out by God and profitable for teaching, for reproof, for correction, and for training in righteousness" (2 Tim. 3:16).

Personal Implications

Take time to reflect on the implications of Proverbs 1:1–7 for your own life today. Consider what you have learned that might lead you to repent of folly, pursue wisdom, and grow in your fear of the Lord. Make notes below on the personal implications for your walk with the Lord of the (1) *Gospel Glimpses*, (2) *Whole-Bible Connections*, (3) *Theological Soundings*, and (4) this passage as a whole.

1. Gospel Glimpses

2. Whole-Bible Connections

3. Theological Soundings

4. Proverbs 1:1–7

> ## As You Finish This Unit . . .

Take a moment now to ask for the Lord's blessing and help as you continue in this study of Proverbs. And take a moment also to look back through this unit of study and reflect on a few key things that the Lord may be teaching you.

Definitions

[1] **Sanctification** – The process of being conformed to the image of Jesus Christ through the work of the Holy Spirit. This process begins immediately after regeneration and continues throughout a Christian's life.

[2] **Word, the** – When spelled with an initial capital letter, can refer to either the written Word of God or Jesus Christ (John 1:1–18).

WEEK 3: A FATHER'S INVITATION TO WISDOM

Proverbs 1:8–7:27

The Place of the Passage

In the first eight chapters of Proverbs we find a series of appeals from a father to his son, or sons, issuing a call to participate in the benefits of a life governed by wisdom. A young man can choose either the path of the wise, which is characterized by the fear of the Lord, or the path of folly, which entails a rejection of God's ways. The paternal appeals in chapters 1–8 set out in poetic form the themes that will appear in the proverbs proper in subsequent chapters.

The Big Picture

In keeping with the mandate of covenant life for God's people, a father passes on to the next generation the truth that the fear of the Lord is the path to wisdom.

Reflection and Discussion

Read through the entire text for this study, Proverbs 1:8–7:27. Then interact with the following questions concerning this section of Proverbs and record your notes on them. (For further background, see the *ESV Study Bible*, pages 1135–1147, or visit esv.org.)

Read Proverbs 1:8–19. This first paternal appeal is a warning against those who promise profit by taking sinful advantage of others. Such plots offer companionship and immediate gain, yet they lead down a path that ends in destruction. The force behind the temptation is greed, what the apostle Paul calls "the love of money" (1 Tim. 6:10). The father concludes his warning by pointing out that accumulating wealth through greed "takes away the life of its possessors" (Prov. 1:19). Considering the passage as a whole, what might this loss of life include?

Proverbs 2:1–22 is one long conditional sentence: "If . . . , then . . ." The protasis, the if-clause, is set out in verses 1–4 and stresses the need to seek diligently after wisdom. Those who do will understand the fear of the Lord and thereby understand God's ways (vv. 5–8). According to verses 6–8, what aspects of God's character will be discovered by those who pursue wisdom? In verses 9–22, how does wisdom benefit those who find it?

The third paternal appeal, Proverbs 3:1–12, provides instruction on how to act in wisdom and teaches that obeying the instruction results in blessing. Verses 3–4 are a call to safeguard covenant life; verses 5–8 teach the necessity of humility, which is firmly anchored here to trusting the Lord; verses 9–10 guide the hearer or reader to acknowledge in practical ways that everything comes from God's hand; and verses 11–12 are a call to submit to God's discipline. Rewards of success, health, and prosperity are held forth for obeying the instruction in this passage. Are these rewards always experienced in tangible ways? How should we best understand them?

The fourth appeal, Proverbs 3:21–35, encourages the one who finds wisdom to guard it, knowing that the Lord sustains and secures the path of the righteous. At the center of the appeal is a series of commands (vv. 27–31) prohibiting actions that violate love of neighbor and incur the Lord's displeasure. The father expresses how God views the wicked: "Toward the scorners he is scornful" (v. 34). Read James 4:6; 1 Peter 5:5–6; and Psalm 138:6. Taken together with Proverbs 3:34, what do these passages reveal about the folly of pride?

The focus of the fifth appeal is the importance of passing down to each generation the nature of covenant life. In Proverbs 4:1–9 the father, after giving an opening encouragement, cites the appeal that his own father made to him. The son is therefore hearing wisdom garnered from the preceding two generations. The boy's grandmother is also mentioned in the passage. How do Deuteronomy 6:4–8; Psalm 78:1–8; Matthew 19:13; and Ephesians 6:1–4 deepen your understanding of the significance of the theme of this passage?

The sixth paternal appeal comes in Proverbs 4:10–19, and it asserts that everyone must make a choice between the way of wisdom and the way of folly. Trace the course of each path in verses 10–19 to its inevitable conclusion. Contrast the images the teacher uses to illuminate the two paths. What terms appear more than once in the passage, and what specifically does this repetition emphasize?

Proverbs 4:20–27 holds the seventh appeal. The emphasis here is on safeguarding oneself on the path of wisdom. Staying on course involves disciplining the heart (v. 23), the tongue (v. 24), the eyes (v. 25), and the feet (vv. 26–27). Read Mark 7:21–23 and Luke 6:45. How do these two Gospel texts show that Proverbs 4:23 is the key verse in this paternal appeal?

The eighth appeal, all of Proverbs 5, concerns matters of sexual morality. The message of the passage is given by illustrating the allure of an immoral woman and the consequences of following her into sin. The wise person is able to adapt the counsel inherent in the illustration wherever applicable to his or her life. What traits do you see in verses 3–6 that are blatantly antithetical to the traits of wisdom put forth in Proverbs thus far? What antidote to temptation is given in verses 15–20?

Proverbs 6:1–19 gives instruction for dealing wisely with people who bear responsibility for their plight. We find a warning against putting up security for another (vv. 1–5), an exhortation of the sluggard to follow the example of the ant lest he come to ruin (vv. 6–11), and a description of the sort of characteristics that the Lord hates (vv. 12–19). This final section begins with a numeric literary device, "There are six things that the LORD hates, seven that are an abomination to him" (v. 16), which indicates that the list is representative rather than exhaustive. What shared aspects are found in the sinful traits listed in verses 17–19, and what negative impact is shared by all?

The ninth and tenth paternal appeals continue the theme of sexual ethics and focus more specifically on adultery. In the ninth appeal, Proverbs 6:20–35, what particular consequence of adultery does the author emphasize? The tenth appeal, all of chapter 7, begins with a warning to keep away from an adulterous woman and then outlines what happens to someone who refuses to resist temptation. What, according to the teacher, is the way of wisdom in avoiding such a downfall? Read 2 Samuel 11. How might this sad incident in Israel's history have shaped the book of Proverbs?

Read through the following three sections on *Gospel Glimpses*, *Whole-Bible Connections*, and *Theological Soundings*. Then take time to consider the *Personal Implications* these sections may have for you.

▶ Gospel Glimpses

THE GIFT OF WISDOM. "For the Lord gives wisdom" (Prov. 2:6a). The opening chapters of Proverbs issue a clear invitation to the reader to pursue, seek after, and obtain wisdom. In fact, it makes clear that seeking wisdom is the essence of wisdom! Yet no matter how diligently we apply ourselves, we are incapable of laying hold of the wisdom we so desperately need, and because that is true, God gives it to us. The gift of wisdom is held out to us by James in the New Testament as well: "If any of you lacks wisdom, let him ask God, who gives generously to all without reproach, and it will be given him" (James 1:5).

DISCIPLINE. God's discipline of his people is linked to his love for them, which is why a father instructs his son, "Do not despise the LORD's discipline or be weary of his reproof, for the LORD reproves him whom he loves, as a father the son in whom he delights" (Prov. 3:11–12). This passage is cited in Hebrews 12, where it is introduced with a question: "Have you forgotten the exhortation that addresses you as sons?" (v. 5). Discipline from the Lord's hand is a sign of his favor and our status in his covenant family.

STEADFAST LOVE AND FAITHFULNESS. A young man is instructed, "Let not steadfast love and faithfulness forsake you" (Prov. 3:3a). This is covenant language, used here as an encouragement to live faithfully with and among God's covenant people. The verse reflects God's self-revelation of his character to Moses: "The LORD, the LORD, a God merciful and gracious, slow to anger, and abounding in steadfast love and faithfulness" (Ex. 34:6). The fullest picture of God's steadfast love was demonstrated in the life and death of his Son, Jesus.

▶ Whole-Bible Connections

TWO PATHS. "The path of the righteous is like the light of dawn, which shines brighter and brighter. . . . The way of the wicked is like deep darkness" (Prov. 4:18–19). The doctrine of the two ways, or paths, is found throughout Scripture, and it is the underlying message of Proverbs. There is the way of wisdom and the way of folly, the path of covenant life and relationship with God and the path of idolatry.[1] The two paths and their inevitable outcomes are portrayed in Psalm 1; the prophet Jeremiah called the good way the "ancient" path (Jer. 6:16). Later, Jesus made known that he himself is the good way, the path to eternal life, and he described it as "narrow" (Matt. 7:14). Following that, the apostle Paul sets out the opposing ways of law and grace: "Now we are released from the law, having died to that which held us captive, so that we serve in the new way of the Spirit and not in the old way of the written code" (Rom. 7:6). Ultimately, wisdom teaches us that through our submitting to God and trusting him, he will guide our feet along the right path (Prov. 3:5–6).

ADULTERY. Much space in Proverbs is devoted to the topic of sexual sin, most specifically adultery. The covenant of marriage was instituted by God at creation (Gen. 2:24–25) and serves as an earthly representative of God's covenant relationship with his people, most fully in believers' union with Christ. Given the sacred nature of marriage, the law prescribed death as the penalty for adultery (Lev. 20:10). Adultery is closely linked to idolatry in Scripture; to worship idols is to commit spiritual adultery against God and forsake one's covenant relationship with him (Jer. 3:9; 5:7; Ezek. 23:37; Hos. 4:13; Rev. 2:20–22).

THE HEART. "Keep your heart with all vigilance, for from it flow the springs of life" (Prov. 4:23). "Heart" in Proverbs regularly refers to the center of one's inner life and orientation to God, from which persons do all their thinking, feeling, and choosing. Jesus echoed Moses when he told a scribe that the first and greatest commandment is to love God with all one's heart (Mark 12:29–30; see Deut. 6:4–5), and there are many references, most especially in the Psalms, to offering to God wholehearted love. To be less than fully committed to the Lord is, according to James, to be double-minded: "Draw near to God, and he will draw near to you. Cleanse your hands, you sinners, and purify your hearts, you double-minded" (James 4:8).

Theological Soundings

JUDGMENT.[2] "They shall eat the fruit of their way, and have their fill of their own devices" (Prov. 1:31). The ultimate judgment for rejecting God and his ways and pursuing an unrepentant course of sin is to be given over to the sin itself. God eventually lifts his gracious restraints. We find a fuller picture of this hardening process in Romans 1, where Paul outlines the downward spiral of those "who by their unrighteousness suppress the truth" (Rom. 1:18). Paul repeatedly declares that God gives them over in increasing degrees to a debased mind and the practice of evil (vv. 24–32).

ELECTION.[3] "For the LORD gives wisdom" (Prov. 2:6). Proverbs invites us to share in the blessings of wisdom, which is to enjoy fellowship with God and his people, yet apart from God's intervention, we remain fools, scorners, scoffers, and haters of knowledge. That is why, for all the many appeals in Proverbs to seek after and acquire wisdom, ultimately we receive it only because God gives it to us. The same holds true of eternal salvation, as Paul writes: "By grace you have been saved through faith. And this is not your own doing; it is the gift of God" (Eph. 2:8).

Personal Implications

Take time to reflect on the implications of Proverbs 1:8–7:27 for your own life today. Consider what you have learned that might lead you to praise God, repent of sin, and trust in his gracious promises. Make notes below on the personal implications for your walk with the Lord of the (1) *Gospel Glimpses*, (2) *Whole-Bible Connections*, (3) *Theological Soundings*, and (4) this passage as a whole.

1. Gospel Glimpses

2. Whole-Bible Connections

3. Theological Soundings

4. Proverbs 1:8–7:27

As You Finish This Unit . . .

Take a moment now to ask for the Lord's blessing and help as you continue in this study of Proverbs. And take a moment also to look back through this unit of study and reflect on a few key things that the Lord may be teaching you.

Definitions

[1] **Idolatry** – In the Bible, usually refers to the worship of a physical object. Paul's comments in Colossians 3:5, however, suggest that idolatry can include covetousness, since it is essentially equivalent to worshiping material things.

[2] **Judgment** – Any assessment of something or someone, especially moral assessment. The Bible also speaks of a final day of judgment when Christ returns, when all those who have refused to repent will be judged (Rev. 20:12–15).

[3] **Election** – In theology, God's sovereign choice of people for redemption and eternal life. Related to the doctrine of predestination.

WEEK 4: WISDOM PERSONIFIED

Proverbs 8:1–36

The Place of the Passage

Proverbs 8 continues the opening section of the book, the purpose of which is to instruct the young and simple to embrace wisdom and to persevere on its path. In this chapter, wisdom is personified as a woman, a literary device that occurs also in 1:20–33 and again in Proverbs 9. Although the structure of chapter 8 differs from the preceding chapters, the appeal in verse 32, "And now, O sons, listen to me," shows this chapter to be a continuation of the introductory section.

The Big Picture

Proverbs 8 points to the covenant Lord as not only the source of all wisdom but also the creator of all that exists.

▶ Reflection and Discussion

Read through the complete passage for this study, Proverbs 8:1–36. Then review the questions below and write your notes on them concerning what the call of Lady Wisdom reveals about God. (For further background, see the *ESV Study Bible*, pages 1148–1149, or visit esv.org.)

"Does not wisdom call? Does not understanding raise her voice?" (8:1). In Proverbs 8:1–5 wisdom is portrayed as readily available. Lady Wisdom places herself at the most traversed area of the community: "beside the gates in front of the town" (v. 3; compare 1:21). Gates were the center of civic and economic life in an Israelite city, where the leading men gathered. Two rhetorical questions (a literary device) open this section (8:1). How do these questions nuance the appeal in the verses that follow?

Lady Wisdom describes the character of her words as noble and right (Prov. 8:6), truthful (v. 7), and righteous (v. 8); then in 8:9 she says, "They are all straight to him who understands, and right to those who find knowledge" (8:9). How might her truth be perceived as straight? Conversely, how might it appear as crooked or twisted to those who won't embrace it?

Read Psalm 73 (esp. vv. 1–3, 25) and 1 John 2:15–17 along with Proverbs 8:10–11. Based on these passages, what sort of desires can so easily mute the voice of wisdom?

"The fear of the LORD is hatred of evil" (Prov. 8:13a). Describing what wisdom hates (and therefore what the Lord hates) calls us to examine our heart, to guard it in the ways of wisdom, to walk in accord with what the Lord loves, and to seek wisdom for every aspect of life. What aspects of Lady Wisdom's appeal in Proverbs 8, along with those in the appeals of Proverbs 1–7, work to instill a hatred of evil in students of wisdom?

"The LORD possessed me at the beginning of his work, the first of his acts of old" (Prov. 8:22). The verse means that wisdom is part of the character of God, and by it he created the world. In 8:22–31 God's creating activity is set forth poetically through the eyes of Lady Wisdom. She was there "like a master workman" (v. 30) and rejoiced in the way God ordered the world to function (vv. 30–31). In other words, everything in creation operates continually through wisdom. What does this teach about the practical benefits of obtaining wisdom for day-to-day life?

Read John 1:1–3; 1 Corinthians 1:18–31; Colossians 1:16–17; and Hebrews 1:3, 10–12 along with Proverbs 8:22–31. Taken together, what do these passages reveal about Christ? (For further background on personified wisdom and Christ, see the *ESV Study Bible*, pages 1132–1133, or visit esv.org.)

"And now, O sons, listen to me" (Prov. 8:32). By addressing "sons," this section not only concludes Wisdom's appeal in verses 1–31 but also draws together all of the paternal appeals as sharing her overall purpose: to extol the benefits of wisdom for faithful covenant living. Review the entire passage (vv. 1–36) and note the rewards offered to those who find wisdom. In light of all that Lady Wisdom promises to those who find her, why would anyone "hate" her (v. 36)?

"Blessed is the one who listens to me, watching daily at my gates, waiting beside my doors" (8:34). What heart attitude is depicted here as necessary for experiencing the blessings of wisdom?

Read through the following three sections on *Gospel Glimpses*, *Whole-Bible Connections*, and *Theological Soundings*. Then take time to consider the *Personal Implications* these sections may have for you.

Gospel Glimpses

WISDOM TO THE UNDESERVING. "O simple ones, learn prudence; O fools, learn sense" (Prov. 8:5). The simple and fools are among those who have not embraced God's ways, yet they are invited to do so and to experience the blessings of his covenant. Lady Wisdom's call to learn finds its ultimate fulfillment in Jesus' call to learn from him: "Come to me, all who labor and are heavy laden, and I will give you rest. Take my yoke upon you, and learn from me, for I am gentle and lowly in heart, and you will find rest for your souls" (Matt. 11:28–29).

SEEKERS REWARDED. "I love those who love me, and those who seek me diligently find me" (Prov. 8:17). The diligence spoken of here is not exhausting mental exercise but rather wholeheartedness and sincerity. Those who humbly seek the Lord in order to know him more fully and to follow his ways will find what they are looking for. When Solomon was young, his father, King David, instructed him to devote his life to this pursuit: "And you, Solomon my son, know the God of your father. . . . If you seek him, he will be found by you" (1 Chron. 28:9); and in Matthew's Gospel Jesus promised reward to seekers: "Ask, and it will be given to you; seek, and you will find; knock, and it will be opened to you" (Matt. 7:7).

LIFE AND FAVOR. Wisdom promises, "Whoever finds me finds life and obtains favor from the LORD" (Prov. 8:35). Lady Wisdom holds out promise for blessings in this life and also points forward to the source of eternal life. To find wisdom is to find Christ, who said, "I am the way, and the truth, and the life. No one comes to the Father except through me" (John 14:6).

Whole-Bible Connections

TREASURE. Wisdom is held out as more valuable than silver, gold, jewelry, or any earthly treasure (Prov. 8:10–11, 18–19). Elsewhere, Isaiah claims that "the fear of the LORD is Zion's treasure" (Isa. 33:6), and the theme is applied to God's kingdom in Jesus' parables (Matt. 13:44–46), where Jesus teaches that gaining the kingdom is worth forsaking all earthly treasure. The apostle Paul exhorted the rich to have an eternal focus, "thus storing up treasure for themselves as a good foundation for the future, so that they may take hold of that which is truly life" (1 Tim. 6:19).

GATES. Lady Wisdom cries at the gates in front of the town (Prov. 8:3). The walled cities of the ancient Near East had covered gatehouses that served as protection from invaders. During times of peace all gates would be open, and the gatehouse would provide a shady place for civic activity. Throughout

Scripture, gates are pictured as a place of separation between those who belong to God and those who do not. Jesus spoke of the narrow gate that leads to life and the wide gate that leads to destruction (Matt. 7:13–14). That is why the psalmist cries, "Open to me the gates of righteousness, that I may enter through them and give thanks to the LORD." (Ps. 118:19). At the end of the age, when Christ Jesus has destroyed rebellious kings and nations, the gates of the New Jerusalem will never be shut because there will be no more hostile invaders (Rev. 21:24–27).

Theological Soundings

CHRISTOLOGY. The way wisdom is portrayed in Proverbs 8 as being integrally present at creation points to the eternal Son of God. In the New Testament we find this same language applied to Christ. Paul wrote that "by him all things were created, in heaven and on earth, visible and invisible, whether thrones or dominions or rulers or authorities—all things were created through him and for him" (Col. 1:16), and John begins his Gospel with the eternality of the Son (John 1:1) and shows him as an agent in creation (John 1:10).

SALVATION. Lady Wisdom claims that she is the way to life and, therefore, to miss her is to love death (Prov. 8:35–36). This foreshadows Jesus Christ as the only source of life, so to reject the Savior is to embrace death and to miss eternal life.[1] We are given this fuller picture in the book of Hebrews: "See that you do not refuse him who is speaking. For if they did not escape when they refused him who warned them on earth, much less will we escape if we reject him who warns from heaven" (Heb. 12:25).

CREATION. Proverbs 8 reveals a facet of God's work in creation that we don't see as clearly in the Genesis 1–3 account, and that is the fact that God wove wisdom into the created order so that it would function as a coherent system. Therefore, those who submit to God and his ways—the wise—are able to participate in the rationality at the heart of created things, which is why Lady Wisdom says that her words "are all straight to him who understands" (8:9).

Personal Implications

Take time to reflect on the implications of Proverbs 8:1–36 for your own life today. Consider what you have learned that might lead you to praise God more fully. Make notes below on the personal implications for your walk with the Lord of the (1) *Gospel Glimpses*, (2) *Whole-Bible Connections*, (3) *Theological Soundings*, and (4) this passage as a whole.

1. Gospel Glimpses

2. Whole-Bible Connections

3. Theological Soundings

4. Proverbs 8:1–36

> ### As You Finish This Unit . . .

Take a moment now to ask for the Lord's blessing and help as you continue in this study of Proverbs. And take a moment also to look back through this unit of study and reflect on a few key things that the Lord may be teaching you.

Definitions

[1] **Eternal Life** – For believers, the new life that begins with trust in Jesus Christ alone for salvation and continues after physical death with an eternity in God's presence in heaven.

WEEK 5: LADY WISDOM AND LADY FOLLY

Proverbs 9:1–18

The Place of the Passage

Proverbs 9:1–18 contains the final poem of the first major section of the book (1:8–9:18). Here we find contrasting personifications of wisdom (9:1–12) and of folly (vv. 13–18), presented as Lady Wisdom and Lady Folly. In the flow of the book, the introduction and this chapter act as bookends (see 1:7 and 9:10) to unify the entire section in its call to recognize, internalize, and walk in the way of wisdom. The key verse at the beginning, "The fear of the LORD is the beginning of knowledge" (1:7), is given similarly here: "The fear of the LORD is the beginning of wisdom" (9:10).

The Big Picture

Proverbs 9:1–18 provides a poetic description of the two paths, wisdom and folly, and strongly encourages the humble to choose the path of wisdom.

Reflection and Discussion

Read through the complete passage for this study, Proverbs 9:1–18. Then review the questions below concerning this section of Proverbs and write your notes on them. (For further background, see the *ESV Study Bible*, pages 1150–1151, or visit esv.org.)

Lady Wisdom invites the simple to her feast (Prov. 9:2–5). All are welcome except scoffers, who the faithful are warned to avoid (9:7). Read Proverbs 13:1; 15:12; and 21:24. What traits make a scoffer unwelcome at wisdom's feast?

How are the scoffer and the wise man contrasted in Proverbs 9:8–9? What heart attitude characterizes the wise, and to what does this lead?

According to Proverbs 9:7–9, what can happen to someone who tries to correct a scoffer? Jesus issued similar guidance, warning his followers not to cast their "pearls" before pigs (Matt. 7:6). Why do you think such a warning is wise? See Acts 13:46 and 18:6.

Proverbs 9:10, "The fear of the LORD is the beginning of wisdom," together with 1:7, serves as the foundation for all the appeals to wisdom in 1:1–9:18, and the expression "fear of the LORD" appears 12 additional times in Proverbs—1:29–31; 2:1–5; 8:13; 10:27; 14:26–27; 15:16, 33; 16:6; 19:23; 22:4; 23:17. Considering these passages together, summarize the aspects of wisdom that characterize those who fear the Lord.

According to Lady Wisdom, "If you are wise, you are wise for yourself; if you scoff, you alone will bear it" (Prov. 9:12). How is this teaching explained by Matthew 12:36; 16:27; Romans 14:12; and Galatians 6:4–5, and in what ways can this teaching serve as a warning to the church today?

Proverbs 9:13–18 pertains to Lady Folly. What traits does she share with the immoral woman of Proverbs 5:3–6; 7:11–12? What do these similarities indicate about the heart of a fool and the dangers a fool poses to the wise?

Both Lady Wisdom and Lady Folly call out to the simple (9:4, 6, 16). What does each hold out to the simple as a reward for following her?

Look back over Proverbs 9:1–18. What differences do you note in how the author of the poem structured his presentations of Lady Wisdom and Lady Folly? For example, note how many verses he devotes to each of the two and the way in which he presents their respective appeals.

Read through the following three sections on *Gospel Glimpses*, *Whole-Bible Connections*, and *Theological Soundings*. Then take time to consider the *Personal Implications* these sections may have for you.

▶ Gospel Glimpses

INVITATION. "Come, eat of my bread and drink of the wine I have mixed" (Prov. 9:5). Lady Wisdom invites the simple and senseless to partake of her feast of wisdom. God offers a similar invitation through the prophet Isaiah, this one to partake of the coming Messiah, wisdom incarnate: "Come, everyone who thirsts, come to the waters; and he who has no money, come, buy and eat! Come, buy wine and milk without money and without price" (Isa. 55:1). Both invitations are offered to those who have nothing to bring to the table except hunger and thirst. This is the heart of gospel grace.

BREAD OF LIFE. Lady Wisdom invites the simple: "Come, eat of my bread and drink of the wine I have mixed" (Prov. 9:5). This finds its ultimate fulfillment in Jesus, who offered himself as bread: "I am the bread of life; whoever comes to me shall not hunger" (John 6:35, 48). He is the living bread who brings eternal life to those who eat (John 6:51). Believers participate in his life-giving feast by partaking of the Lord's Supper.[1] At this new covenant feast, Christ is present spiritually with and in the believing recipients of the bread and wine, strengthening their faith and fellowship in him and thereby feeding their souls (see, e.g., Matt. 26:26–28; 1 Cor. 11:23–26).

▶ **Whole-Bible Connections**

FEASTING. Lady Wisdom invites the simple to sit down at her table and feast, which is symbolic of joy and blessing in God's presence. In the old covenant, God stipulated times for certain feasts, each of which was intended to express God's relationship with his people (see Leviticus 23). The celebration of God's bounty accompanies the feasting in Scripture. In Isaiah, God promises "for all peoples a feast of rich food, a feast of well-aged wine" (Isa. 25:6). Later, Jesus likens the kingdom of heaven to a feast (Matt. 22:2), and during his earthly ministry he provided good wine for a wedding feast (John 2:1–11). In glory, believers will feast at the "marriage supper of the Lamb" (Rev. 19:9).

DOOR. Lady Folly "sits at the door of her house" (Prov. 9:14). Her posture depicts a woman watching and waiting to ensnare the uncommitted as well as the faithful. She brings to mind King David's first wife, Michal, who looked out of her window "and saw King David leaping and dancing before the LORD, and she despised him in her heart" (2 Sam. 6:16). There was also the wicked queen Jezebel, who "painted her eyes and adorned her head and looked out of the window" (2 Kings 9:30). Unlike Lady Folly, who sits at her door, Jesus Christ stands at each person's own door, seeking entry in order to welcome, not destroy, those who embrace him (Rev. 3:20). In John's Gospel, Jesus himself is the door (John 10:7, 9).

SHEOL. "Her guests are in the depths of Sheol" (Prov. 9:18). The idea of going up to heaven[2] at the time of death does not appear often in the Old Testament. More common is the idea of "going down" to Sheol, the world of the dead, which is often pictured as being under the earth (Gen. 37:35; Ps. 6:5; 9:17; Isa. 14:9–20). God is the one who raises up a soul from Sheol (Ps. 30:3), demonstrating his authority over the dead as well as the living. Sometimes Sheol is a synonym for "death," as in 2 Samuel 22:5–6.

▶ **Theological Soundings**

THE CHURCH. "Wisdom has built her house" (Prov. 9:1), into which the covenant community is invited to enter. Jesus, who has become for us wisdom from God (1 Cor. 1:30), is building his house, the church, which is comprised of all those united to him by faith. Believers are likened to living stones that are being built into a spiritual house (1 Pet. 2:2–5; see Heb. 3:6), and as citizens of this living house, of which Jesus Christ is the cornerstone, we together form a dwelling place for God's Spirit (Eph. 2:19–22).

SIN AS DECEPTION. "Stolen water is sweet and bread eaten in secret is pleasant" (Prov. 9:17). Sin has a hardening effect on an unrepentant heart, and the outworking of such a heart is to see evil as beneficial. This is a sign of God's judgment, an indicator of God's giving someone over to his or her evil inclinations (see Rom. 1:18–32). God's judgment in this regard works in tandem with the individual, who is simultaneously giving himself over to his sin (Eph. 4:19). Finding sin to be "sweet" or "pleasant" stands in direct contrast to the fear of the Lord, which leads to hatred of evil (Prov. 8:13).

▶ Personal Implications

Take time to reflect on the implications of Proverbs 9:1–18 for your own life today. Consider what you have learned that might lead you to praise God, repent of sin, and trust in his gracious promises. Make notes below on the personal implications for your walk with the Lord of the (1) *Gospel Glimpses*, (2) *Whole-Bible Connections*, (3) *Theological Soundings*, and (4) this passage as a whole.

1. Gospel Glimpses

2. Whole-Bible Connections

3. Theological Soundings

4. Proverbs 9:1–18

▶ As You Finish This Unit . . .

Take a moment now to ask for the Lord's blessing and help as you continue in this study of Proverbs. Take a moment also to look back through this unit of study and reflect on a few key things that the Lord may be teaching you.

Definitions

[1] **The Lord's Supper** – A meal of remembrance instituted by Jesus on the night of his betrayal. Christians are to observe this meal, also called Communion, in remembrance of Jesus' death. It consists of wine, symbolizing the new covenant in his blood, and bread, symbolizing his body, which was broken for his followers.

[2] **Heaven** – The sky, or the abode of God (Matt. 6:9), which is commonly regarded as being above the earth and sky. As the abode of God, heaven is also the place where believers live in God's presence after death (Luke 23:43).

Week 6: Proverbs of Solomon

Proverbs 10:1–16:33

The Place of the Passage

Here begin the maxims, the "proverbs proper," that are attributed to King Solomon. In this section we find word pictures of how God designed the world to work under his governing authority. The wise seek to understand and live within God's design in day-to-day life, but the fool ignores or outright shuns this wise path. This section shows that wisdom is necessary—and available—for every arena of one's life and relationships.

The Big Picture

In Proverbs 10:1–16:33, Solomon shows how those who live in the fear of the Lord are blessed and how the foolish are cursed.

Reflection and Discussion

Read through Proverbs 10:1–16:33, which will be the focus of this week's study. Following this, review the questions below concerning this section of the book of Proverbs and write your responses. (For further background, see the *ESV Study Bible*, pages 1151–1163, or visit esv.org.)

Read Proverbs 10:1–5. The purpose of these proverbs is to promote righteous practices in one's labors. Taken together with Proverbs 11:28, what is the relationship between wisdom and wealth? See also Jesus' parable of the rich fool in Luke 12:13–21.

"The one who conceals hatred has lying lips" (Prov. 10:18a). Proverbs is filled with contrasts of wise and foolish speech, and lying or liars is a primary emphasis (e.g., 6:19; 12:19, 22; 14:5, 25; 19:5; 21:6). Two proverbs, 10:18 and 26:28, link hatred and lying. In what way might a liar harbor a heart of hatred toward those to whom he lies?

Proverbs 12:15 declares, "The way of a fool is right in his own eyes, but a wise man listens to advice." Several proverbs advocate the wisdom of seeking counsel when planning and before making decisions (see 11:14, 15:22; 20:18; 24:6; compare 18:1). We find that expression, "right in his own eyes," elsewhere in Scripture, most notably during a godless time in Israel's history (Judg. 17:6; 21:25). The term refers to those who do whatever they want as opposed to what the Lord wants. What is indicated by the individual or corporate pursuit of autonomy? (See also Proverbs 18:1.)

Proverbs 13:4 observes, "The soul of the sluggard craves and gets nothing, while the soul of the diligent is richly supplied." The sluggard in Proverbs is not merely someone who is idle but someone who is apathetic or complacent (1:32). He has a negative impact on himself and on the community (10:26). Sluggards are admonished to observe the benefits of diligence (6:6–11), otherwise they live in fear (22:13; 26:13) and suffer a tragic end (21:25; 24:30–34). The importance of diligence is found also in the New Testament. Read 1 Corinthians 9:3–15; 2 Corinthians 11:7–9; and 1 Thessalonians 3:6–12. How is the diligence of a believer advantageous to the spread of the gospel?

Proverbs 13:23 observes one cause of poverty: injustice. In addition to injustice, poverty can be caused by sloth (6:9–11; 28:19), by God's punishment of wickedness (10:2–3; 13:25), or by his mysterious providence (e.g., 22:2). Proverbs makes the case that walking the paths of wisdom leads to blessing, but it does not guarantee material success; in fact, Proverbs also makes the case that an abundance of wealth can lead to folly (30:8). Read Luke 12:13–21 and 2 Corinthians 8:1–9. How is poverty shown to be something God uses to produce spiritual fruit in the lives of his people?

Proverbs 14:15–16 shows that the wise person gives thought to his path and turns away from evil. In contrast, the fool is reckless (14:16b). God holds people accountable for their thoughts (Isa. 55:7; Jer. 4:14; Matt. 9:4; 12:25), which come from the heart (Matt. 15:19; Mark 7:21). Based on Romans 12:2; 2 Corinthians 10:3–5; and Hebrews 4:12, how does one's mind function in the process of sanctification?

Read Proverbs 14:17, 29; 15:18; and 16:32 (see also 19:11). One who is slow to anger reflects God's character (Ex. 34:6). In what ways does a quick temper reveal folly? See Matthew 18:21–35; Galatians 5:19–20; Ephesians 4:31; and James 1:19–20.

Proverbs 16 contains three verses that clearly show God's sovereign intervention in the affairs of mankind (vv. 1, 3, 33). What enables someone to know God's providential rule as comforting rather than frustrating?

Four things in Proverbs are called a "fountain of life": a righteous tongue (10:11), wise teaching (13:14), the fear of the Lord (14:27), and good sense

(16:22). How are these four aspects of wisdom shown more fully in the new covenant? See John 4:1–14; 7:37–39.

Read through the following three sections on *Gospel Glimpses, Whole-Bible Connections*, and *Theological Soundings*. Then take time to consider the *Personal Implications* these sections may have for you.

▶ Gospel Glimpses

DESIRE FULFILLED. "The desire of the righteous will be granted" (Prov. 10:24). The idea is that those who desire wisdom will be given wisdom. God delights to satisfy the heart that longs for him. The psalmist declares that those who take delight in the Lord will be given the desires of their heart (Ps. 37:4), and Asaph, after steadying his gaze on God, was able to declare that nothing on earth could satisfy his desire like God (Ps. 73:25). The longing for wisdom, righteousness, and primarily God himself is one that is guaranteed to be satisfied (Matt. 5:6; 1 John 5:14–15).

ATONEMENT.[1] "By steadfast love and faithfulness iniquity is atoned for" (Prov. 16:6). God's very nature is one of love and mercy. He portrayed himself this way to Moses (Ex. 34:6), and this aspect of his character—steadfast love and faithfulness—is echoed in Psalms (25:10; 61:7; 86:15; 89:14; 98:3) and the rest of the Old Testament (Num. 14:18; Deut. 5:10; 2 Chron. 30:9; Neh. 9:17; Dan. 9:4; Joel 2:13). The sin of God's people is forgiven solely because God loves, the ultimate expression of which was shown at the cross of Jesus Christ. Proverbs 16:6 points forward in history to this sacrifice of God's Son, proving once and for all that his steadfast love and faithfulness have atoned for the sin of his people.

DELIVERANCE. "The righteous is delivered from trouble, and the wicked walks into it instead" (Prov. 11:8). The proverb underscores the general principle that those who live by the fear of the Lord avoid much trouble. However, the faithful are not exempt from all the difficulties of life, and none obtains a righteousness sufficient to navigate all of life's hardships. Human beings need a deliverance and a righteousness beyond what they can provide for themselves. Such a deliverer has been provided for us in the person of Jesus Christ, by whose righteousness we are delivered. Upon his return, at his second coming, we will fully and finally be delivered from all of life's hardships.

Whole-Bible Connections

CHILDREARING. Raising children in the fear of the Lord is mandated throughout Scripture, and an aspect of childrearing, physical discipline, is a common theme in Proverbs (see, e.g., Prov. 10:13; 17:10; 22:15; 23:13–24; 29:15). It is viewed as an important part of teaching children to avoid wrong behavior, to embrace what is right, and to build godly character. Children who grow up to fear the Lord bring honor to their parents (10:1; 15:20; 29:3). In the New Testament, well-trained children serve as an indicator of parental godliness; a criterion for leadership in the church is the behavior of one's children (1 Tim. 3:4, 12). At the same time, parents are warned against provoking their children to anger (Eph. 6:4). Much of the biblical instruction in this regard is directed to children themselves (see Ex. 20:12; Prov. 1:8; 6:20; 23:22; and Eph. 6:1–2).

THE TONGUE. "The mouth of the righteous brings forth wisdom, but the perverse tongue will be cut off" (Prov. 20:31). Since the tongue can produce either death or life, the wise person will guard his or her speech. This is a prevalent theme in Proverbs. One reveals by his words whether he is wise or foolish, and that is because the words one utters spring from the heart, as Jesus made clear (Matt. 12:34; 15:18–19; Luke 6:45). James's epistle includes an entire section on the tongue, and, echoing Proverbs, James claims that one's words direct the course of one's life (James 3:1–12).

PRIDE. "The LORD tears down the house of the proud" (Prov. 15:25a). The scoffer in Proverbs is someone characterized by pride. The proud are self-exalting rather than God-exalting, and because of that, they scorn the path of wisdom. In the New Testament, also, we see that God stands opposed to the proud, who are unable to receive grace (James 4:6, 10; 1 Pet. 5:5). Both James and Peter cite Proverbs 3:34 to make their case: "Toward the scorners he is scornful, but to the humble he gives favor."

Theological Soundings

OMNISCIENCE. "The eyes of the LORD are in every place, keeping watch on the evil and the good" (Prov. 15:3; compare 5:21; 22:12). God is omniscient, which means that he sees and knows all. God's omniscience is an "incommunicable attribute" of his character, which means it is an attribute that he does not share with human beings. For that reason, the fact of God's omniscience is hard for us to grasp. In Scripture, the term "eyes of the Lord" is used to express God's judging or discerning between good and evil (e.g., Gen. 6:8; 2 Sam. 15:25; 2 Chron. 14:2; Zech. 4:10) as well as his care and concern for his people, as in Psalm 34:15.

DIVINE PROVIDENCE.[2] Not only the careful plans of the heart (Prov. 16:1, 9) but even the apparently random practice of casting lots falls under God's providential governance (Prov. 16:33). God is sovereign over everything that comes to pass. Jesus said God rules even things that man deems insignificant, using as an example the fact that not even a bird falls to the ground without God's consent (Matt. 10:29). Included in the sphere of God's sovereignty is the salvation of individual sinners (see Rom. 9:1–21), although this does not negate human responsibility. God uses human actions and choices to fulfill what he has ordained. With regard to tragedies and evil, the biblical writers never blame God for them (see Rom. 5:12; 2 Tim. 4:14; also Job 1:21–22). Rather, they see the doctrine of God's sovereignty as a means of comfort and assurance, confident that evil will not triumph and that God's good plans for his people will be fulfilled. How God's sovereignty and human responsibility work together in the world is a mystery that no one can fully understand.

KINGSHIP. "It is an abomination to kings to do evil, for the throne is established by righteousness" (Prov. 16:12). Proverbs 16:10–15 has to do with kingship. Verses 10 and 12 seem to represent the king as flawlessly wise, especially since he is descended from King David. Jesus Christ is the ultimate king, the one whom all the Davidic kings foreshadowed, so no human being can assume kingship except as a deputy of the divine King. According to Genesis, all human beings were created as "royal" figures in the image of God to rule and control other creatures for the sake of the King of the universe. So when God allowed the people of Israel to have a human king (1 Sam. 8:6–9), he gave them a king only as God's earthly vice-regent or deputy, responsible to the Lord for his actions and subject to his commands (see esp. 1 Sam. 12:14; 2 Sam. 12:9).

▶ **Personal Implications**

Take time to reflect on the implications of Proverbs 10:1–16:33 for your life today. Consider what you have learned that might lead you to praise God and repent of sin. Make notes below on the personal implications for your walk with the Lord of the (1) *Gospel Glimpses*, (2) *Whole-Bible Connections*, (3) *Theological Soundings*, and (4) this passage as a whole.

1. Gospel Glimpses

2. Whole-Bible Connections

3. Theological Soundings

4. Proverbs 10:1–16:33

> ### ▶ As You Finish This Unit . . .

Take a moment now to ask for the Lord's blessing and help as you continue in this study of Proverbs. And take a moment also to look back through this unit of study and reflect on a few key things that the Lord may be teaching you.

Definitions

[1] **Atonement** – The reconciliation of a person with God, often associated with the offering of a sacrifice to pay the penalty for sin and appease the wrath of God. Through his death and resurrection, Jesus Christ made atonement for the sins of believers.

[2] **Providence** – God's good, wise, and sovereign guidance and control of all things, by which he supplies all our needs and accomplishes his holy will.

Week 7: More Proverbs of Solomon

Proverbs 17:1–22:16

The Place of the Passage

This lesson continues with more proverbs attributed to King Solomon. Solomon provided word pictures of the way in which God designed the world to work under his governing authority. The wise seek to understand and live within God's design in day-to-day life, but the fool ignores or shuns this wise path. This section shows that wisdom is necessary—and available—for every arena of one's life and relationships.

The Big Picture

In Proverbs 17:1–22:16, Solomon shows how those who live in the fear of the Lord are blessed and how the foolish are cursed.

▶ Reflection and Discussion

Read through the complete passage for this study, Proverbs 17:1–22:16. Then review the questions below concerning this section in the book of Proverbs and write your notes on them. (For further background, see the *ESV Study Bible*, pages 1164–1173, or visit esv.org.)

We find in Proverbs 17:20–22 three things that will bring sorrow to the heart: a crooked and dishonest life (v. 20), a foolish son (v. 21), and too much discouragement (v. 22). In what way does this observation fit into the main thesis of Proverbs (compare 2 Cor. 7:10)?

Proverbs 17:27–28 points out that one trait of wisdom is restrained speech. The opposite is also true—hasty, thoughtless speech is associated with folly (29:20). What other speech patterns mentioned in this section of Proverbs might reveal someone as either foolish or wise? See Proverbs 17:14, 20; 18:2, 4, 8, 13; 19:5, 9; 20:3, 19, 25; 21:28.

Proverbs 18:23–19:4 observes misfortune from various angles, one of which involves companionship. A few friends stick by someone even in bad times (18:24), but the great majority of one's companions stay close by only as long as one's fortunes are good; in bad times, they disappear (19:4; see Ps. 38:11; 41:9; 55:12–14). Wisdom comes, first, in recognizing this reality in a fallen world and, second, in responding to it in the fear of the Lord. How do Jeremiah 17:5; John 15:14–15; and James 2:22–23 define that response?

Proverbs 19:2 states that "desire without knowledge is not good." This could refer to an impulsive person who acts unwisely before properly thinking or planning. It could also indicate that there is folly in giving free rein to desires that are not governed by the fear of the Lord. How can God's people rule their desires with wisdom? See Psalm 73 (esp. v. 25); Proverbs 8:11; 10:24; 18:1; 1 Corinthians 14:1; Philippians 1:23; 1 Timothy 6:9; James 1:14–15; 4:1–4; 1 John 2:16–17.

"When a man's folly brings his way to ruin, his heart rages against the LORD" (Prov. 19:3). People often blame God for their misfortune when they should be blaming themselves. According to Hebrews 3:12–19, why is it wise to consider Proverbs 19:3 as a warning?

"Haughty eyes" in Proverbs is a term used for pride and is mentioned as something the Lord considers to be an "abomination" (Prov. 6:16–17; 16:5). The thing most likely to bring divine judgment on one's head is pride (21:4), which most characterizes a scoffer (21:24). Consider the overall picture of a scoffer in

Proverbs (1:22; 9:7–8; 13:1; 14:6; 15:12; 22:10; 24:9). From this picture, how is pride manifested in one's life and heart?

"The king's heart is a stream of water in the hand of the LORD; he turns it wherever he will" (Prov. 21:1). The Lord is the King of kings, and therefore every governing body is under his authority and control. How is the king as depicted in Proverbs a reflection of the King of kings? See 16:10–15; 20:8, 28; 24:21; and 29:14.

"He who loves purity of heart, and whose speech is gracious, will have the king as his friend" (Prov. 22:11). The proverb is making the observation that transparent integrity makes one trustworthy and endows him with a good reputation. More importantly, the pure in heart are blessed by and with God (Ps. 73:1; Matt. 5:8). What, according to Psalm 111:1; 119:2, 10, 34; Jeremiah 24:7; Romans 8:5; James 4:8; and 1 Peter 1:22, begets a pure heart and issues from it?

Proverbs 22:7 observes, "The rich rules over the poor, and the borrower is the slave of the lender." The rich of verse 7 are set in contrast to the generous of verse 9, who share their wealth with the poor. The wisdom to obtain from 22:7a is clear: one who fears the Lord cares for the downtrodden. What practical wisdom can be gleaned from the observation in the second part of the verse (22:7b)?

Read through the following three sections on *Gospel Glimpses, Whole-Bible Connections*, and *Theological Soundings*. Then take time to consider the *Personal Implications* these sections may have for you.

Gospel Glimpses

REFUGE. "The name of the LORD is a strong tower; the righteous man runs into it and is safe" (Prov. 18:10). The truth of this verse is set in contrast to verse 11, which talks about the danger of seeking security in wealth. Only the Lord is a secure refuge in times of trouble and, most importantly, a refuge from the consequences of sin. The writer of Hebrews says that those "who have fled for refuge" to Jesus Christ as their mediator find him to be a "sure and steadfast anchor of the soul" (Heb. 6:18–19).

FAITHFULNESS. "Many a man proclaims his own steadfast love, but a faithful man who can find?" (Prov. 20:6). People's pretenses of virtue are often false, and even where virtue is proven, it falls far short of God's standard, which is perfection. Where can true goodness be found? That is the question posed by the proverb. Ultimately, no human being meets God's standard of faithfulness, something Jesus experienced while he walked this earth (John 2:24–25). Only Christ satisfies our quest for someone to trust utterly (Heb. 3:6).

JOY. "A joyful heart is good medicine" (Prov. 17:22a). Joy is meant to be characteristic of covenant life. Joy characterizes the Psalms, as the covenant community worships God together (e.g., 5:11; 16:11; 21:6; 32:11; 35:27; 63:7; 132:9). Such joy isn't circumstantial and can be experienced even amid great suffering. The cross of Christ represents the greatest suffering in history, for Jesus not only suffered physically but also experienced God's just wrath in taking upon himself the sin of the world. Still, the promise of future reward and joy gave Jesus strength to suffer (Heb. 12:2). The apostle Paul was characterized by joy even while suffering in prison, and that was because his whole purpose for living was Christ (Phil. 1:21). Believers grow in joy as they are increasingly transformed into the likeness of Christ by the work of the Holy Spirit (Gal. 5:22) and as they seek to rejoice in the Lord in all things (Phil. 4:4).

▶ Whole-Bible Connections

ABOMINATION. Several things in Proverbs are pictured as an "abomination" in God's eyes: a devious person (Prov. 3:32); a false balance or unequal weights (11:1; 20:10, 23); a crooked heart (11:20); lying lips (6:17, 19; 12:22); one who sows discord among brothers (6:19); the sacrifice, the way, and the thoughts of the wicked (15:8–9, 26; 21:27); haughty eyes or an arrogant heart (6:17; 16:5); devising evil (6:18); winking at evil and condemning righteousness (17:15). The term is also important in the book of Deuteronomy. It denotes a significant sin, often with the sense of social or theological hypocrisy, and God's increased anger against it. Daniel prophesied about "the abomination that makes desolate" (Dan. 11:31–32). Several times in Jewish history it was thought that this prophecy was being fulfilled, but Jesus clarifies that the complete fulfillment of Daniel's prophecy will be found in (1) the Roman destruction of the temple in AD 70 (see Matt. 24:15) and (2) the image of the Antichrist[1] being set up in the last days (see 2 Thess. 2:4; Rev. 13:14).

MARRIAGE. "He who finds a wife finds a good thing and obtains favor from the LORD" (Prov. 18:22). This verse refers to both the human action and the divine governance of a marital relationship, while Proverbs 19:14 states that a wise wife is specifically a gift from God. Marriage was instituted by God at creation (Gen. 2:24), and it serves as a reflection of the covenant relationship between God and his people. In the Old Testament, Israel is frequently depicted as God's "bride" (e.g., Isa. 62:4–5; Jer. 2:2; Hos. 2:16–20), and in the New Testament John the Baptist calls Jesus the bridegroom (John 3:29), which identifies Jesus as Israel's long-awaited King and Messiah. The fullest picture of human marriage as a picture of the union of Christ and believers is found in Ephesians 5:22–33.

THE POOR. "Whoever closes his ear to the cry of the poor will himself call out and not be answered" (Prov. 21:13). God has a tender heart toward the poor (Isa. 41:17). He commands his people to show compassion and alleviate their suffering (Deut. 15:11), and the prophets spoke out against abuses of those exploited in their poverty (e.g., Isa. 3:15; Ezek. 22:29; Amos 2:7; Zech. 7:10). While poverty will always be a fact in this fallen world (Deut. 15:11; Matt. 26:11; Mark 14:7; John 12:8), the church reflects the compassion of God by meeting the practical needs of the poor, beginning with the poor in the church (Rom. 15:26;

Gal. 2:10). James had scathing remarks for believers who cultivate the wealthy for personal gain yet ignore the poor (James 2:1–6).

Theological Soundings

JUDGMENT. "The crucible is for silver, and the furnace is for gold, and the LORD tests hearts" (Prov. 17:3). God alone knows the hearts of individuals (Jer. 17:10), and he often exposes what is harbored in someone's heart by means of adversity, which is depicted in this proverb by the terms "crucible" and "furnace." We find similar imagery in Malachi, where God is like a "refiner's fire" (Mal. 3:2). The image stresses both thoroughness and severity. The heat of a refiner's fire was intense in order to separate dross from pure metal. When God's people undergo such testing, it should be understood as God's fatherly discipline: trials work to purify the hearts of believers, conforming them to the image of Christ (Heb. 12:7–11).

WRATH. "A king's wrath is like the growling of a lion, but his favor is like dew on the grass" (Prov. 19:12). The proverb does not say that a king's anger (or favor) is always right, but that it is powerful. God's wrath, on the other hand, is always perfectly just. The anger of human authority can serve as a warning to unrepentant sinners to turn from their sin and embrace the righteous king (Rom. 13:1–4). One day it will be too late to avert the Lord's wrath (Rom. 2:5, 8; Rev. 6:16–17). God's people, however, have been destined for salvation, not wrath (1 Thess. 5:9), and are being delivered from God's wrath by the Lord Jesus (Rom. 5:9; 1 Thess. 1:10).

Personal Implications

Take time to reflect on the implications of Proverbs 17:1–22:16 for your life today. Consider what you have learned that might lead you to trust in his gracious promises. Make notes below on the personal implications for your walk with the Lord of the (1) *Gospel Glimpses*, (2) *Whole-Bible Connections*, (3) *Theological Soundings*, and (4) this passage as a whole.

1. Gospel Glimpses

2. Whole-Bible Connections

3. Theological Soundings

4. Proverbs 17:1–22:16

As You Finish This Unit . . .

Take a moment now to ask for the Lord's blessing and help as you continue in this study of Proverbs. And take a moment also to look back through this unit of study and reflect on a few key things that the Lord may be teaching you.

Definitions

[1] **Antichrist** – This term, appearing only in the epistles of John (e.g., 1 John 2:18), describes anyone who firmly denies that Jesus is the Christ, the unique Son of God. John and other NT writers may also have foreseen the appearance of one particular "Antichrist" in the end times. The one Paul describes as the "man of lawlessness" (2 Thess. 2:3–4) may be that person.

WEEK 8: SAYINGS
OF THE WISE

Proverbs 22:17–24:34

▲

The Place of the Passage

This section reflects an awareness of an Egyptian wisdom text titled *The Instruction of Amenemope* and dated to about 1250 BC. The most significant difference between the two is the devotion to the Lord exhibited in Proverbs. The identity of "the wise" (Prov. 22:17) to whom the proverbs are attributed is unknown; they might be the scholars who assembled these proverbs (possibly under Solomon's sponsorship).

The Big Picture

This collection of sayings establishes that the fear of the Lord undergirds all true wisdom and the way in which it is practiced in daily life.

> ### Reflection and Discussion

Read the entire text for this week's study, Proverbs 22:17–24:34. Then review the following questions concerning this section of Proverbs and write your notes on them. (For further background, see the *ESV Study Bible*, pages 1173–1178, or visit esv.org.)

A purpose of imparting wisdom, says the wise man in Proverbs 22:19, is to deepen trust in God, which is a vital component of what it means to fear the Lord. In what ways does the obtainment of wisdom serve to deepen trust? See also Proverbs 3:1–2, 5–8.

Proverbs stresses that one aspect of wisdom is discernment in friendship. We find this not only in this section of Proverbs but sprinkled throughout the collection as a whole. Review the proverbs that touch on this topic: 17:17; 18:24; 19:4, 6; 22:11, 24–25; 27:6, 9, 17. What practical wisdom is advocated for choosing friends, and what warnings are given? What should the wise avoid?

Proverbs 22:25 teaches that a bad attitude toward life and people is contagious and deadly. We find this truth elsewhere in Scripture (see, e.g., Num. 13:1–14:4). Included in the biblical teaching is the danger not only of bad attitudes but also of sinful acts. The apostle Paul stressed that when publicly known sin is not dealt with, it can spread its destructive consequences throughout the whole fellowship (1 Cor. 5:6–7; 15:33). Of the character types we have encountered thus far in Proverbs, which ones are most likely to be destructively contagious?

Proverbs 22:29 observes that one skillful in his labors will be recognized for his skill. The implied exhortation is that one should never be careless about the quality of one's work. The apostle Paul gave a similar exhortation in Philippians, instructing believers to focus on things that are commendable and excellent and to imitate Paul himself in this regard (Phil. 4:8–9). Why is excellence in one's work an aspect of wisdom?

"Do not toil to acquire wealth; be discerning enough to desist," says Proverbs 23:4. The discernment advocated here is supplied in the next verse: "When your eyes light on it, it is gone, for suddenly it sprouts wings, flying like an eagle toward heaven" (v. 5). What does this teach about a wise outlook on wealth? See also Proverbs 15:27; Matthew 6:19–21; 1 Timothy 6:9–10; and Hebrews 13:5.

What is set in contrast to envy in Proverbs 23:17? Why are the two mutually exclusive? This section contains more instruction about envy (24:1, 19), and the topic is addressed also in the first section (3:31). Each instance advises a young man not to be envious of the wicked. Why might this be a temptation? What is the remedy for envy? See Psalms 37:1–2 and 73:1–28.

"Partiality in judging is not good" (Prov. 24:23b). This begins the second portion, "Further Sayings of the Wise," of this lesson. Proverbs 24:23–26 focuses on justice in court. Courts must render honest verdicts, convicting the guilty and acquitting the innocent. People may be prejudiced for or against people because they are rich and famous or of a certain race, but partiality of any kind is to be rejected. In what other realms of day-to-day life might the sin of partiality creep in? Read James 2:1–13. What is the "royal law" that showing partiality violates?

Proverbs 24:27 encourages sensible preparation before building a house, so that one may attend well to the life lived in it. Jesus uses this idea in Luke's Gospel as an analogy for discipleship (Luke 14:25–33). Whether the consideration is practical, as in Proverbs, or spiritual, as in Luke, what wisdom is being advocated in this teaching?

Proverbs 24:28–29 instructs against taking revenge. This principle was included in the Mosaic law (Lev. 19:18). God's people are instructed to refrain from revenge because God's justice will eventually rain down in destruction on unrepentant sinners (Deut. 32:34–36; Rom. 12:19; Heb. 10:29–31). Concerning revenge, another aspect of God's character is revealed by Jesus in Matthew 5:43–48. How does a person's refusal to engage in vengeful activity reflect wisdom as well as the heart of God?

Read through the following three sections on *Gospel Glimpses*, *Whole-Bible Connections*, and *Theological Soundings*. Then take time to consider the *Personal Implications* these sections may have for you.

Gospel Glimpses

REDEEMER. "Do not move an ancient landmark or enter the fields of the fatherless, for their Redeemer is strong; he will plead their cause against you" (Prov. 23:10–11). The reference to orphans suggests that the victims may be too weak to defend themselves against those who treat them unjustly, but the good news is that they have a Redeemer who comes to their aid. The proverb points us to our Redeemer, Jesus Christ, who comes to the rescue of people held in subjection to sin. As our mediator,[1] he pleads our case before the divine Judge, having offered himself as a once-for-all sacrifice for the salvation and perfection of all his followers (Heb. 9:14–15).

REJOICING. "My son, if your heart is wise, my heart too will be glad" (Prov. 23:15). The father speaking here is motivated to teach by love, and his joy is in seeing his son succeed in life. At a much deeper level, this reflects divine joy in the salvation of the lost. Jesus told a parable about a man who seeks his lost sheep in order to make this point: "I tell you, there will be more joy in heaven over one sinner who repents than over ninety-nine righteous persons who need no repentance" (Luke 15:3–7).

HOPE. Wisdom is compared to honey, a delightful treat that is sweet to the taste, and for those who find it, "there will be a future, and [their] hope will not be cut off" (Prov. 24:13–14). This promise of hope is the essence of the gospel—a future and a hope—and it is the Lord's gift to all who trust in him for salvation (see Jer. 29:11). Hope is imparted to believers by the Holy Spirit (Rom. 15:13) and also through their sufferings (Rom. 5:3–5), and it is tied inextricably to the future (1 Cor. 15:12–58; 2 Cor. 1:9–10; Heb. 10:23; 1 Pet. 1:3–5, 13).

> ## Whole-Bible Connections

LANDMARKS. "Do not move the ancient landmark that your fathers have set" (Prov. 22:28; compare 23:10). The proverb echoes the law given to Moses (Deut. 19:14; 27:17). Moving the landmark, or boundary stone, of a neighbor was tantamount to theft of land. The law emphasized keeping land in families, since inheritance rights were basic to Israel's daily life. Land-grabbing violated the divine intention that all of God's people were to enjoy their inheritance, and it created a wealthy, power-abusing class that incurred God's anger (Hos. 5:10). In the New Testament, the inheritance of God's people has been obtained through Christ, and it is preserved for them in heaven (1 Pet. 1:3–5).

EARS TO HEAR. The opening verse of this section calls on people to incline their ears to hear words of wisdom (Prov. 22:17). In Scripture, inclining the ear or having ears to hear means to listen intently and with one's heart. God's people frequently began prayers of petition by asking God to incline his ear (e.g., 2 Kings 19:16; Ps. 31:2; 71:2; 86:1; 102:2; Isa. 37:17; Dan. 9:18), and the Lord appeals for his people's attention in the same way (e.g., Isa. 55:3; Matt. 11:15; Mark 4:9; Luke 8:8; Rev. 2–3).

DRUNKENNESS. "The drunkard and the glutton will come to poverty, and slumber will clothe them with rags" (Prov. 23:21). This section of Proverbs contains an exposition on the folly of drunkenness, and it depicts the very real consequences of alcohol abuse (23:29–35; see Luke 21:34). Wine is seen as a blessing in Scripture (Gen. 27:28; Ps. 104:15), and it factored into celebratory occasions (John 2:1–10), but drunkenness is soundly condemned (Gal. 5:19–21; Eph. 5:18; 1 Thess. 5:6–8), and strong drink was forbidden to priests on duty and to those set apart for special service to God (Lev. 10:9; Num. 6:1–4). The dulling of the conscience brought about by drunkenness leads to additional sins (see Gen. 9:20–27; 19:32–35; Rom. 13:13).

> ## Theological Soundings

PERSEVERANCE OF THE SAINTS. "The righteous falls seven times and rises again" (Prov. 24:16a). The righteous is able to rise repeatedly because both his person and his path are sustained by the Lord. God's people are called to persevere in faith and obedience, and their doing so confirms their status in God's covenant family (Heb. 6:9–12). Although believers are tempted by sin and at times succumb to those temptations, they are kept secure by the power of God

(Jude 24–25). God will never let his own fall away but will keep them by his grace (John 6:37, 39; 10:27–29; Rom. 8:28–39; Phil. 1:6).

GOD'S WORD. "Incline your ear, and hear the words of the wise, and apply your heart to knowledge, for it will be pleasant if you keep them within you" (Prov. 22:17–18a). The words offered by the sage can impart wisdom to the reader, give him practical skills for dealing with people, and encourage the fear of the Lord. These words are transformative at a much deeper level, since they are actually God's words, part of Scripture (Heb. 4:12). God's Word is the primary means employed by the Holy Spirit to effect spiritual growth and Christlikeness in the lives of believers (Eph. 6:17). The longest psalm in the Psalter, Psalm 119, celebrates the gift of God's Word, and its goal is to enable God's people to admire his Word so strongly that they will work hard and pray to have it shape their character and conduct.

> ## Personal Implications

Take time to reflect on the implications of Proverbs 22:17–24:34 for your life today. Consider what you have learned that might lead you to praise God, repent of sin, and trust in his gracious promises. Make notes below on the personal implications for your walk with the Lord of the (1) *Gospel Glimpses*, (2) *Whole-Bible Connections*, (3) *Theological Soundings*, and (4) this passage as a whole.

1. Gospel Glimpses

2. Whole-Bible Connections

3. Theological Soundings

4. Proverbs 22:17–24:34

> ### As You Finish This Unit . . .

Take a moment now to ask for the Lord's blessing and help as you continue in this study of Proverbs. And take a moment also to look back through this unit of study and reflect on a few key things that the Lord may be teaching you.

Definitions

[1] **Mediator** – One who intercedes between parties to resolve a conflict or achieve a goal. Jesus is the only mediator between God and rebellious humanity (1 Tim. 2:5).

Week 9: Hezekiah's Collection of Proverbs

Proverbs 25:1–29:27

▲

Proverbs 25–29 contains proverbs collected under the leadership of King Hezekiah of Judah. The present form of the book of Proverbs came into existence, at the earliest, in the reign of Hezekiah (715–686 BC). He was a king who "did what was right in the eyes of the LORD" (2 Kings 18:3). Hezekiah is credited with reviving Judah's religious traditions, and a new edition of Solomonic proverbs was apparently part of that revival. In this collection there are groupings of proverbs that focus, among other things, on the king, the fool, and the sluggard.

The Big Picture

Proverbs 25:1–29:27 continues the themes of practical wisdom found throughout the book, revealing the sort of life that is lived in the fear of the Lord and exposing the sort that rejects it.

> ### Reflection and Discussion

Read through the complete text for this study, Proverbs 25:1–29:27. Then review the questions below concerning this portion of Proverbs and write your notes on them. (For further background, see the *ESV Study Bible*, pages 1178–1186, or visit esv.org.)

The wise teacher instructs, "Do not put yourself forward in the king's presence or stand in the place of the great, for it is better to be told, 'Come up here,' than to be put lower in the presence of a noble" (Prov. 25:6–7). What virtue is the teacher advocating? Conversely, what vice is he rebuking? Read James 4:6 and 1 Peter 5:5 (both of which quote the teaching of Proverbs 3:34). What in these passages takes the instruction of Proverbs 25:6–7 beyond simply building a good reputation among men?

Proverbs 25:9–10 gives instruction on how best to resolve relational conflict: "Argue your case with your neighbor himself" (v. 9a). The concern here is safeguarding one's reputation (v. 10). Read Matthew 18:15–17. How does Jesus build on this teaching? What is Jesus' ultimate objective?

"With patience a ruler may be persuaded, and a soft tongue will break a bone" (Prov. 25:15). What quality is being praised in this proverb, and what paradox is put forth? See also 15:1 and 16:14, 32. What dimension is added in 1 Peter 3:15–16?

One aspect of wisdom is knowing how to act appropriately in the situation at hand, which is the point of Proverbs 25:20: "Whoever sings songs to a heavy heart is like one who takes off a garment on a cold day, and like vinegar on soda." Jesus exemplified the wisdom contained here during his ministry. His words and actions fit each person and circumstance perfectly; he did not employ a "one size fits all" approach. How can this wisdom inform our witness to those around us? What might hinder such an approach? See also Romans 12:15.

The wise teacher observes, "A man without self-control is like a city broken into and left without walls" (Prov. 25:28). Self-control is necessary to govern the passions, the appetites, and the will. The sage illustrates his point with imagery that his students would readily have understood. Ancient cities were fortified by high walls as a means of defense; if those walls were breached, the residents of the city were vulnerable to destruction. What sort of enemies can attack someone who lacks self-control? What blessing do new covenant believers have in this regard? See Galatians 5:16–24.

Proverbs 25:28–26:12 is a set of proverbs that focuses primarily on the fool. Part of being wise is learning how to recognize and respond to a fool. One identifying mark of a fool is his unwillingness to learn and change: "Like a dog that returns to his vomit is a fool who repeats his folly" (26:11), a proverb the apostle Peter cited to describe those who turn away from God and back toward the world (2 Pet. 2:22). What other traits of folly are revealed in this set of proverbs, and how should the wise respond?

Proverbs 26:13–16 focuses on the sluggard. Verses 13–15 present him as comically ludicrous in his laziness. What trait is attributed to the sluggard in verse 16, and how does this trait broaden the wise person's understanding of how a lazy person thinks?

This section of Proverbs describes the destructive effects of a sinful tongue. A "whisperer" or gossip is mentioned in Proverbs 26:20, 22. Twice in Proverbs gossip is likened to "delicious morsels that go down into the inner parts of the body" (18:8; 26:22). What is the implicit warning in those words? Proverbs 26:24, 28 mentions lying. What does lying reveal about the heart of a liar?

"Do not boast about tomorrow, for you do not know what a day may bring" (Prov. 27:1). The first two verses of Proverbs 27 concern boasting. In verse 1, a person should not boast of his prospects; in verse 2, he should not boast of himself. Read James 4:13–14. How does James reveal boasting as folly?

"The prudent sees danger and hides himself, but the simple go on and suffer for it" (Prov. 27:12; also 22:3). Based on the overall teaching in Proverbs examined thus far, what sort of danger or dangers do the wise hide from? See also 1 Corinthians 6:12–18 and 10:1–14.

Proverbs 28:19–27 concerns the desire to secure prosperity and favor for oneself. The teaching begins, "Whoever works his land will have plenty of bread, but he who follows worthless pursuits will have plenty of poverty" (v. 19). The teacher is condemning get-rich-quick schemes. Why are such schemes condemned, and what lies in the heart of those who consistently pursue them? See 1 Timothy 6:6–10.

Read through the following three sections on *Gospel Glimpses*, *Whole-Bible Connections*, and *Theological Soundings*. Then take time to consider the *Personal Implications* these sections may have for you.

▶ Gospel Glimpses

FAITHFUL MESSENGER. Proverbs 25:13 likens a faithful messenger to cooling weather in the extreme heat of harvest time: both provide needed refreshment (see 13:17). The prophets, however, spoke of a future messenger, one who would bring news of eternal refreshment (Isa. 40:3; Mal. 3:1), and Jesus confirmed that the fulfillment of that prophecy was the person of John the Baptist, the messenger who prepared the way for Jesus Christ (Matt. 3:1–3; Mark 1:1–3; Luke 1:76–79). The Baptist brought the news of what the Messiah would do: "give light to those who sit in darkness and in the shadow of death, and . . . guide our feet into the way of peace" (Luke 1:79).

MERCY. "Whoever conceals his transgressions will not prosper, but he who confesses and forsakes them will obtain mercy" (Prov. 28:13; see 1 John 1:6–9). People aren't accepted by God because they confess and forsake their sin; rather, confession of sin and repentance accompany salvation, which is first a gift from God. God's mercy toward his people always precedes their holy response, and that is because his righteous wrath toward sin was completely satisfied at the cross of Jesus. God's very nature is one of mercy (Ex. 34:6), and because of the atonement we are invited to approach him and appeal to him for it (Heb. 4:16). Confession of sin and repentance are a mark of God's covenant people, those who have received mercy.

▶ Whole-Bible Connections

REFINER'S FIRE. "Take away the dross from the silver, and the smith has material for a vessel" (Prov. 25:4). Similar imagery occurs in Scripture to describe God's sovereign work in the lives of his people (Jer. 18:4; Rom. 9:21), and it is a fit metaphor for the way in which the Lord sanctifies his people through hardship (Heb. 12:7–11).

MUDDIED SPRING. Proverbs 25:26 likens a man who compromises his convictions to "a muddied spring or a polluted fountain." The image of muddy water is found also in Ezekiel, where God condemns the greedy behavior of his people (Ezek. 34:18–19). Jesus criticized the church at Laodicea for being lukewarm, and because they were neither hot nor cold, he threatened to spit them out of his mouth (Rev. 3:15–16). Both cold and hot water are useful: cold water refreshes in the heat, and hot water is a medicinal tonic. Jesus found his church's tepid indifference utterly distasteful.

HARDENED HEART. "Blessed is the one who fears the LORD always, but whoever hardens his heart will fall into calamity" (Prov. 28:14). A hardened heart is one that continually and wholeheartedly rejects the Lord and his ways. In Scripture we see that the hardening process is the work of both God and the individual, most notably in the case of Pharaoh in Exodus (e.g., 4:21; 7:3; 8:15; 9:12, 34; 10:20). The apostle Paul uses the account of Pharaoh to explain God's sovereignty in salvation, concluding that God "has mercy on whomever he wills, and he hardens whomever he wills" (Rom. 9:1–18). In so doing, Paul is affirming that God ordains all that happens, even though God himself does not sin and is not responsible for a person's sin. Although God is the authoritative agent in the hardening of a heart, God's people are warned to be actively on guard over the state of their heart (Heb. 3:7–12).

Theological Soundings

GOD CONCEALS. "It is the glory of God to conceal things, but the glory of kings is to search things out" (Prov. 25:2). The king's searching is part of his role under the overall governance of God, who keeps some things hidden or secret (Deut. 29:29). Even if all was revealed, the depths of God—his wisdom, knowledge, judgments, and ways—are beyond human comprehension. The apostle Paul praises God for his transcendence: "Oh, the depth of the riches and wisdom and knowledge of God! How unsearchable are his judgments and how inscrutable his ways!" (Rom. 11:33).

IDOLATRY. "The fear of man lays a snare, but whoever trusts in the LORD is safe" (Prov. 29:25). One who acts primarily out of a fear of people shows that he does not trust the Lord to preserve and protect him. By "fear of man," the sage has in mind the conviction that one's well-being is determined by the approval or blessing of human beings. Although we don't find the term "fear of man" used elsewhere in Scripture, we find the idea throughout, and it is linked to idolatry. In his prophecy Jeremiah paints a sharp contrast between the paths of those who fear the Lord and those who fear people (Jer. 17:5–10).

Personal Implications

Take time to reflect on the implications of Proverbs 25:1–29:27 for your life today. Consider what you have learned that might lead you to praise God and repent of sin. Make notes below on the personal implications for your walk with the Lord of the (1) *Gospel Glimpses*, (2) *Whole-Bible Connections*, (3) *Theological Soundings*, and (4) this passage as a whole.

1. Gospel Glimpses

2. Whole-Bible Connections

3. Theological Soundings

4. Proverbs 25:1–29:27

As You Finish This Unit . . .

Take a moment now to ask for the Lord's blessing and help as you continue in this study of Proverbs. And take a moment also to look back through this unit of study and reflect on a few key things that the Lord may be teaching you.

WEEK 10: THE SAYINGS OF AGUR AND THE WORDS OF KING LEMUEL

Proverbs 30:1–31:9

The Place of the Passage

Proverbs 30 contains the sayings of Agur, son of Jakeh. His identity is unknown, and his name occurs nowhere else in the Bible. Notable about Agur's words is the stress he lays on humility. Proverbs 31:1–9 contains the words of King Lemuel based on teaching he received from his mother about wise kingship. No one knows who Lemuel was or where he was king. Most suppose that he was not an Israelite.

The Big Picture

In Proverbs 30:1–31:9, the instruction of two otherwise unknown sages expands the scope of what it means to fear the Lord and to reflect his glory in one's calling.

> ### Reflection and Discussion

Read through the complete passage for this study, Proverbs 30:1–31:9. Then review the questions below on this section of Proverbs and record your notes and reflections. (For further background, see the *ESV Study Bible*, pages 1186–1189, or visit esv.org.)

The words of Agur exude humility. First, Agur confesses that he is not learned in wisdom (Prov. 30:2–3), and then he asks a series of rhetorical questions (v. 4). What is the answer to these rhetorical questions, and how do they convey Agur's humility?

In Proverbs 30:15–16 Agur makes an observation about the nature of insatiable cravings. Leeches, fire, Sheol (the place of the dead), and land are dependent for their existence on a continual intake of what feeds them. A woman's womb, however, does not seem to fit the category in quite the same way. What point might Agur have been making by including the barren womb in his observation? See Genesis 30:1.

"Two things I ask of you; deny them not to me before I die" (Prov. 30:7). Agur's petition is the only prayer in the book of Proverbs. What two things does Agur request? In verse 9 he elaborates on his second request. Based on this elaboration, what does Agur value most?

"The leech has two daughters: Give and Give" (Prov. 30:15). How does Agur's observation in verse 15 stand in stark contrast to his prayer in verses 8–9? See also Philippians 4:11–13; 1 Timothy 6:6–10; and Hebrews 13:5.

"This is the way of an adulteress: she eats and wipes her mouth and says, 'I have done no wrong'" (Prov. 30:20). The adulteress's meal is symbolic of her life of adultery. She is of the opinion that nothing remains of the sexual encounter and there are no moral ramifications to her behavior. Agur is describing a seared conscience—one that has become hardened, immune to the conviction of sin. Read Romans 14:1–12; 1 Corinthians 8:1–13; 10:23–30; 1 Timothy 1:18–20; Hebrews 10:19–22. What role does the conscience play in one's growth in holiness? Of what must we be careful concerning the conscience? Is it infallible?

"Under three things the earth trembles; under four it cannot bear up" (Prov. 30:21). In this way Agur introduces a list of four unbearable things: a slave who becomes a king, a well-fed fool, a shrew of a wife, and one who usurps author-ity. How does the list in 30:21–23 compare to that in 30:24–28?

Agur provides a list of paradoxes in Proverbs 30:24–28. Some creatures are small and seemingly insignificant, yet they do surprisingly wise things. Much of God's revelation comes through paradoxes, which he delights to use. Name the paradoxes revealed in 1 Samuel 16:6–13; Matthew 16:25; Luke 1:46–55; Acts 9:1–16; and Philippians 2:5–11. What does each paradox reveal about God and his kingdom?

Proverbs 31:2–9 paints a picture of an ideal king, one set apart in the service of God for the good of God's people. How did the history of King Solomon, under whose authority Proverbs was compiled, perhaps influence the inclusion of this passage in the collection? See 1 Kings 11:1–8.

In King Lemuel's recounting of the oracle his mother taught him, discern-ment concerning strong drink is a feature (Prov. 31:4–7). While it is not wise for kings to imbibe, wine is advocated for those who are suffering. In light of Scripture's condemnation of over-imbibing, how can we best understand this proverb? See Ecclesiastes 3:9–13; 1 Timothy 4:1–5.

Read through the following three sections on *Gospel Glimpses, Whole-Bible Connections*, and *Theological Soundings*. Then take time to consider the *Personal Implications* these sections may have for you.

▶ Gospel Glimpses

SHIELD AND REFUGE. "He is a shield to those who take refuge in him" (Prov. 30:5b). This is warfare imagery. Shields were necessary as a defense for those going into battle; they could protect and provide refuge against attackers. We need a shield and a refuge from our greatest enemy—sin—and we have both, in and through Jesus Christ. He is the Christian's refuge from sin and Satan, and he has already won the battle. Through him, believers can wield the shield of faith and extinguish all the flaming darts of the Evil One (Eph. 6:16).

A GOOD KING. Proverbs 31:2–9 gives instruction about what the ideal human king ought to be like: careful in his personal life (vv. 3–4) so that he may serve and protect others through justice (vv. 5, 9) and compassion (vv. 6–8). This description of a godly king runs contrary to ordinary experience, now as in Bible times, where power is often pursued and used to the gain of the king himself rather than for the sake of those he is leading. That is why this description points us to the gospel—it shows the need for another kind of king (see Isa. 9:6–7). No human king can so ideally fulfill the role; people need a leader who governs beyond human capacities. Jesus came to be our king, but because he did not seem like a king by earthly standards, he was scorned and beaten by those who mocked, "Hail, King of the Jews!" (Matt. 27:29). But now he reigns as King, and he will be King forever (Rev. 15:3; 17:14; 19:16).

WASHED CLEAN. "There are those who are clean in their own eyes but are not washed of their filth" (Prov. 30:12). Every human being needs cleansing, but only those who acknowledge this truth can find it. In Jesus' day, the Pharisees[1] sought cleanliness by meticulously keeping God's law, and they convinced themselves that they could do so and thus be righteous. However, while seeking external purity, the Pharisees were oblivious to the corrupt internal condition of their hearts. Jesus shattered their illusion, saying, "You blind Pharisee! First clean the inside of the cup and the plate, that the outside also may be clean" (Matt. 23:26). And to his disciples he said, "If I do not wash you, you have no share with me" (John 13:8). Jesus is the one—the only one—who can wash us clean, and he has done so (1 Cor. 6:11; Heb. 10:22; Rev. 7:14; compare Zech. 3:1–5).

Whole-Bible Connections

BARRENNESS. "Three things are never satisfied . . . the barren womb . . ." (Prov. 30:15–16). The lack of an heir was a major problem in the ancient Near East. Without an heir, a family line could not continue. This potential hardship deepens the angst expressed in the proverb. Barrenness is not uncommon in the narrative of redemptive history. Beginning with Abraham's wife, Sarah, there were many women, most notably some in the ancestry of Jesus, who longed to birth children but could not conceive or were made to wait before conceiving (see Gen. 11:30; 25:21; 29:31; 1 Sam. 1:2; Luke 1:36). Barrenness also pictured the lack of fruitfulness of God's people under the old covenant, but it was turned into a sign of hope: "'Sing, O barren one, who did not bear; break forth into singing and cry aloud, you who have not been in labor! For the children of the desolate one will be more than the children of her who is married,' says the LORD" (Isa. 54:1).

KINGSHIP. The instructions for kings in Proverbs 31:2–9 showcase the kind of king that was rare in Israel. When God's people first demanded a king to rule over them, they were warned that such leaders would constantly face the temptation to abuse their power for the sake of personal gain. That is exactly what happened. Saul, the first king, was a failure (1 Sam. 15:26–31, 35). David, the second king, brought blessing to the nation until he fell into sin (2 Samuel 11), and though he repented, the remainder of his reign was flawed. David's son Solomon was in some ways a model king, but his decline into sin (1 Kings 11), the sins of his offspring, the division and strife between Israel and Judah, and the continual problems with false worship indicated the need for a perfect king. Some good kings followed, most notably Hezekiah and Josiah, but for the most part, all the kings, both bad and good, pointed to the need for the coming perfect king, King Jesus.

Theological Soundings

GOD'S WORD. "Every word of God proves true" (Prov. 30:5a; see Ps. 18:30). The proverb underscores the truthfulness, trustworthiness, and reliability of the Bible, and we see in it the doctrine of the "plenary" (full, complete) inspiration of Scripture, extending even to "every word." That is why the next verse, 30:6, warns against adding to God's words. The command against altering God's words was initially given by Moses (Deut. 4:2; 12:32), and Jesus similarly warns that those who add to or take away from God's words will incur God's wrath (Rev. 22:18–19).

GOD'S WISDOM. In Proverbs 30:24–28 Agur observes four things that are small but wise (v. 24). Ants are small and weak, but they are instinctively wise; likewise the rock badger is weak but is able to provide a home for himself. Locusts have no leader, yet they exhibit cooperation with one another. The fourth thing is the lizard, an inglorious creature that winds up in glorious places. God's wisdom as explained by the apostle Paul is reflected in this portion of Agur's teaching. Paul wrote that God chooses what is foolish in the world to shame the wise, what is weak to shame the strong, and what is low and despised to bring down the proud (1 Cor. 1:27–31). The epitome of this "wisdom" is a crucified Messiah, a blessed paradox that the worldly wise cannot comprehend.

Personal Implications

Take time to reflect on the implications of Proverbs 30:1–31:9 for your life today. Consider what you have learned that might lead you to praise God more fully. Make notes below on the personal implications for your walk with the Lord of the (1) *Gospel Glimpses*, (2) *Whole-Bible Connections*, (3) *Theological Soundings*, and (4) this passage as a whole.

1. Gospel Glimpses

2. Whole-Bible Connections

3. Theological Soundings

4. Proverbs 30:1–31:9

As You Finish This Unit . . .

Take a moment now to ask for the Lord's blessing and help as you continue in this study of Proverbs. And take a moment also to look back through this unit of study and reflect on a few key things that the Lord may be teaching you.

Definitions

[1] **Pharisee** – A member of a popular religious/political party in NT times characterized by strict adherence to the law of Moses and also to extrabiblical Jewish traditions. The Pharisees were frequently criticized by Jesus for their legalistic and hypocritical practices. The apostle Paul was a zealous Pharisee prior to his conversion.

Week 11: An Alphabet of Womanly Excellence

Proverbs 31:10–31

The Place of the Passage

Proverbs 31:10–31 is set in the form of an acrostic, in which each verse begins with the successive letter of the Hebrew alphabet. The poem is most likely an anonymous contribution and not the work of King Lemuel, whose oracle precedes it (vv. 1–9). The acrostic portrays an ideal woman and shows young men what kind of woman to seek for marriage. The poem begins and ends in the same way—with the value of an excellent wife. However, the woman's marital status is not the primary emphasis of the acrostic. She is a portrait of feminine wisdom. She embodies in all areas of life the full character of wisdom commended in Proverbs.

The Big Picture

Proverbs 31:10–31 shows us that true wisdom is not just for men but for all God's people.

Reflection and Discussion

Read through Proverbs 31:10–31, the passage for this week's study. Then review the following questions, taking notes on the final section of Proverbs. (For further background, see the *ESV Study Bible*, pages 1189–1191, or visit esv.org.)

"The heart of her husband trusts in her, and he will have no lack of gain" (31:11). In what ways does the woman in this poem depict a wife who can be trusted?

What teaching from Proverbs is seen in the depiction of the woman as active from before sunrise till long after sundown? See also Ephesians 5:15–16 and Colossians 4:5.

"She considers a field and buys it; with the fruit of her hands she plants a vineyard" (Prov. 31:16). As you look at what occupies the woman's time, what attitude about her work is different from the prevailing attitude of working women today?

"She dresses herself with strength" (Prov. 31:17). That the woman "dresses herself with strength" means that she covers herself with it. The wording here seems to indicate something more than physical prowess. As you examine her life in the poem, what sort of strength is most likely meant?

The woman in the poem is depicted as confident (Prov. 31:21, 25). From the poem overall, identify two or three things that are the basis for her confidence.

The woman in the poem exemplifies nurturing. No matter what task she is involved in, her primary aim is the nurture of others. She provides food for those in her home, including the servants (Prov. 31:15); she extends her hand to the poor and needy (v. 20); and she watches over the ways of her household (v. 27). How is this nurturing aspect of her character demonstrated in her words (v. 26)?

The acrostic of Proverbs 31:10–31portrays a family of solid financial means. What teachings from Proverbs are reinforced by this portrayal?

Read through the following three sections on *Gospel Glimpses, Whole-Bible Connections,* and *Theological Soundings.* Then take time to consider the *Personal Implications* these sections may have for you.

▶ Gospel Glimpses

HEIRS OF GOD'S BLESSINGS. Males have dominated the illustrations in Proverbs up to now, so the inclusion of the poem of womanly excellence demonstrates that the teaching of the entire book is intended for all God's people. The fullness of this is realized in Christ, in whom "there is neither Jew nor Greek, there is neither slave nor free, there is no male and female, for you are all one in Christ Jesus" (Gal. 3:28). All who are in Christ are heirs of all the riches of God's kingdom, one of which is wisdom.

SECURITY. "Strength and dignity are her clothing, and she laughs at the time o come" (31:25). The main message of Proverbs 10:10–31 is that living in the fear of the Lord results in blessings, one of which is confidence in the Lord's care. Such confidence is enriched by the gospel, because the gospel offers eternal security. Believers can "laugh at the time to come" because they are guarded by God's power (1 Pet. 1:3–5) for the time when God "will wipe away every tear from their eyes, and death shall be no more, neither shall there be mourning, nor crying, nor pain anymore, for the former things have passed away" (Rev. 21:4).

▶ Whole-Bible Connections

FINE LINEN. "Her clothing is fine linen and purple" (Prov. 31:22b). In the ancient Near East, garments of fine linen were worn by the wealthy, but in Scripture fine linen has deeper connotations. At God's instruction, the garments of the high priest were to be made from fine linen (Exodus 28; 39). Also, fine linen was worn by King David and the Levites when they brought the ark of the Lord up to Jerusalem (1 Chron. 15:25–27). Mordecai, who uncovers a plot to kill the Jews and thereby aids in saving them, is afterward clothed with a fine linen robe (Est. 8:15). In Ezekiel's oracle, God enters into a love covenant with his people and then beautifies them with fine linen (Ezek. 16:8–11). However, God's beautified people would soon break that covenant. Yet God prevails, and by Christ's victory his people will again be clothed in fine linen, which, this time, is an indicator of purity and "the righteous deeds of the saints" (Rev. 19:8).

FAMILY. "Her children rise up and call her blessed; her husband also, and he praises her" (Prov. 31:28). In a loving family, the members recognize the value of each other. Here the children and the husband offer their praise. God places a high premium on family. The whole course of redemptive history is built on the family structure, which began when God instructed his people to be fruitful and multiply (Gen. 1:28). In the old covenant, God built a people for himself by means of human procreation (Gen. 15:1–6). In the new covenant the emphasis is on building God's spiritual family through union with Christ, yet the biological family retains its high value (see, e.g., John 19:26–27; Eph. 5:22–6:4; Titus 2:3–5; 1 Pet. 3:1–7).

▶ Theological Soundings

GOD'S GLORY. The overall picture of the poem is that those who fear the Lord are blessed and become a blessing to others, and the result is that God is glorified. God is zealous for his own glory. When people follow God's ways and are blessed for it, he is glorified. The pinnacle of wisdom is to hold God's glory as the theme of one's life and the joy of one's heart. By living in God's ways, God's people are increasingly transformed into the image of Christ, thereby undoing the distortion to that image that occurred at the fall[1]: "We all, with unveiled face, beholding the glory of the Lord, are being transformed into the same image from one degree of glory to another" (2 Cor. 3:18).

MARRIAGE AND GOD'S SOVEREIGNTY. "An excellent wife who can find?" (Prov. 31:10a). The poem begins with a rhetorical question, the answer to which is that only God can bring a woman to a man (see 19:14). God prearranges marriages, as can be seen in how he provided a wife for Isaac (Genesis 24) and a kinsman-redeemer[2] husband for Ruth (Ruth 3–4).

▶ Personal Implications

Take time to reflect on the implications of Proverbs 31:10–31 for your own life today. Consider what you have learned that might lead you to praise God, repent of sin, and trust in his gracious promises. Make notes below on the personal implications for your walk with the Lord of the (1) *Gospel Glimpses*, (2) *Whole-Bible Connections*, (3) *Theological Soundings*, and (4) this passage as a whole.

1. Gospel Glimpses

2. Whole-Bible Connections

3. Theological Soundings

4. Proverbs 31:10–31

As You Finish This Unit . . .

Take a moment now to ask for the Lord's blessing and help as you continue in this study of Proverbs. And take a moment also to look back through this unit of study and reflect on a few key things that the Lord may be teaching you.

Definitions

[1] **Fall, the** – Adam and Eve's disobedience of God by eating the fruit from the tree of the knowledge of good and evil, resulting in their loss of innocence and favor with God and the introduction of sin and its effects into the world (Genesis 3).

[2] **Kinsman-redeemer** – In OT times, a relative in each extended family who had the responsibility to redeem—that is, to buy back—any relative's land in danger of being sold because of debt (Lev. 25:25). In the book of Ruth, Boaz accepted this responsibility (Ruth 4:9–10).

WEEK 12: SUMMARY AND CONCLUSION

We will conclude our study of Proverbs by summarizing the big picture of God's message through Proverbs as a whole. Then we will consider several questions in order to reflect on various Gospel Glimpses, Whole-Bible Connections, and Theological Soundings throughout the entire book.

The Big Picture of Proverbs

The primary theme of Proverbs, "The fear of the LORD is the beginning of wisdom, and the knowledge of the Holy One is insight" (9:10; compare 1:7), is as applicable to God's people today as it was in Solomon's day. The wisdom that grows from the fear of the Lord is displayed in practical ways in covenant life and relationships. In the covenantal framework of Proverbs, wisdom is skill in the art of godly living.

The first major section of Proverbs, 1:8–9:18, instructs the young and the simple to embrace wisdom. A series of poems is designed to instill in the teachable the desire to discern and persevere in the path of wisdom. In two lengthy poems, Proverbs 8–9, wisdom is personified as a great lady. In chapter 8 Lady Wisdom places herself with God at creation, which is a poetic way of pointing to the Lord as the maker of heaven and earth. In chapter 9 Lady Wisdom invites the simple to a banquet of wisdom. Lady Folly also makes an appearance in this poem, and her destructive ways serve as a stark contrast to those of Lady Wisdom.

The proverbs of Solomon are the next major section of the book (10:1–22:16). This section consists primarily of short maxims that reveal how to live wisely within the structure God has established for the world. Some of these individual proverbs are grouped together into small collections that, taken together, give the reader a more complete understanding of a given topic.

The final section includes wisdom instruction in similar themes, although most of the authors of these proverbs are found nowhere else in Scripture. The book concludes with an anonymous acrostic poem that depicts the life of a godly woman, one who fears the Lord. Taken altogether, God's wisdom is held forth to all who are teachable, both men and women, and it will be obtained by the humble seeker.

Read through the following three sections on *Gospel Glimpses*, *Whole-Bible Connections*, and *Theological Soundings*. Then take time to consider the *Personal Implications* these sections may have for you.

▶ Gospel Glimpses

True wisdom comes from God and his instruction, which anticipates the fact that Christ is the wisdom of God (1 Cor. 1:30; Col. 2:3) and that in him and his instruction we find the way of life and righteousness (John 14:6, 23–24). The call of Lady Wisdom in chapters 8–9 prefigures the call of the gospel, and the path of righteousness held forth through the entire book is ultimately that of Jesus Christ, the perfectly righteous one.

Were there any particular passages or themes in Proverbs that gave you a fresh understanding and grasp of God's grace to us through Jesus?

▶ Whole-Bible Connections

The flow of redemptive history is poetically depicted in Proverbs in several aspects. One is the theme of two paths—the path of the wise, which leads to life, and the path of the scoffer, which leads to death. All through Scripture God's people are called to embrace either him or idols, to choose either life or death, to walk in righteousness or in sin. The theme of godly kingship, seen especially in exercising justice, is woven into Scripture from early in the history of God's people. Finally, the excellent wife of Proverbs 31:10–31 finds her fulfillment in the church, the bride of Christ.

How has this study of Proverbs filled out your understanding of the biblical storyline of redemption?

Were there any themes emphasized in Proverbs that helped you to deepen your grasp of the Bible's unity?

Have any passages or themes expanded your understanding of the redemption that Jesus provides, which he began at his first coming and will consummate at his return?

What connections between Proverbs and the New Testament were new to you?

Theological Soundings

Proverbs has much to contribute to Christian theology. Many doctrines and themes are developed, clarified, and reinforced throughout Proverbs, such as the sovereignty of God, the sinfulness of humanity, the eternality of the Trinity, and God's righteousness.

Has your theology shifted in minor or major ways during the course of studying Proverbs? How so?

How has your understanding of the nature and character of God been deepened throughout this study?

What unique contributions does Proverbs make toward our understanding of who Jesus is and what he accomplished through his life, death, and resurrection?

What, specifically, does Proverbs teach us about the human condition and our need of redemption?

Personal Implications

God wrote the book of Proverbs to transform us. As you reflect on Proverbs as a whole, what implications do you see for your life?

What implications for life flow from your reflections on the questions already asked in this week's study concerning *Gospel Glimpses*, *Whole-Bible Connections*, and *Theological Soundings*?

What have you learned in Proverbs that might lead you to praise God, turn away from sin, and trust more firmly in his promises?

As You Finish Studying Proverbs . . .

We rejoice with you as you finish studying the book of Proverbs! May this study become part of your Christian walk of faith, day by day and week by week throughout all your life. Now we would greatly encourage you to continue to study the Word of God on a week-by-week basis. To continue your study of the Bible, we would encourage you to consider other books in the *Knowing the Bible* series, and to visit www.knowingthebibleseries.org.

Lastly, take a moment again to look back through this book of Proverbs, which you have studied during these recent weeks. Review again the notes that you have written, and the things that you have highlighted or underlined. Reflect again on the key themes that the Lord has been teaching you about himself and about his Word. May these things become a treasure for you throughout your life—which we pray will be true for you, in the name of the Father, and the Son, and the Holy Spirit. Amen.